Our Good and Perfect Love Story

Nobody Thought Our Marriage Would Last

Dana E. McKee

By Dana E. McKee

To Pebbles + Mickey, good friends.

Also by Dana E. McKee

Children's book

A is for Ape

Much of the material for this book originally appeared in my blog on WordPress in 2013 and 2014.

Copyright 2022 by Dana E. McKee
Second Edition

Cover design by Daniel M. Wright of CreatedWright

ISBN: paperback 978-1-5136-9509-9, ebook 978-1-5136-9593-8

Library of Congress Cataloging-in-Publication Data
McKee, Dana E., 1953-

Our Good and Perfect Love Story; Nobody Thought Our Marriage Would Last / Dana E. McKee

Summary: Dana Grim Babb wedded Roger McKee and almost immediately found marriage impossibly difficult. Though the decision to leave their home did not seem right to her, no biblical grounds having damaged the covenant, she left. Through counsel and God's help, the couple found love, reunited, and eventually made a good, stable home for themselves and their children.

All the stories in this book are true.
Some of the names have been changed to protect the privacy of those involved.

Photo credit goes to my friend, Brian Mullhollen, for shooting the wedding photograph used on the back cover.

Front cover photos taken by the author.

I dedicate this book to all who jump into life

by committing to marriage.

Come on in; the water's…

turbulent.

But our mighty Savior knows how to calm the storm.

God's peace be yours.

And strength and joy and wisdom.

And love.

Table of Contents

Acknowledgements

I first want to thank Roger for his complete support of my book project. I started writing down our crazy and beautiful story more than twenty years ago. Now, as I draw near to publication, my husband still gives me license to write about personal things. Well, he did say that I go into unnecessary detail in one story. But that one stays in! And you'll never guess which one. (Hint: it involves cleaning a school. And it highlights my groom's one remaining weakness.)

Thanks to those of our kids and grandkids, friends and brothers who read through this. Ben, you remembered that the junker car was not a Volvo, but an Audi. And you provided other details. All of you encouraged me. Thanks for the high fives. And constructive criticisms. Barnabas, Bria, Ariel and Sam; Ray and Douglas; Ruthie, Carol and Carleen…I so appreciate your timely, helpful input. There are others…thank you.

I love you all.

My line editor, Stephanie Nickel, suggested alternative wording, turning around my backwards expressions or misplaced modifiers, and she corrected punctuation in the manuscript, etc., all to make it more coherent. Good calls.

I'm glad I hired you, Stephanie. You gave great advice and pointed out mistakes. I hate mistakes. Thank you, again. (In my last-minute additions after your edit, I probably made and missed a few more blunders. I hope they're small ones.)

Thank you, Daniel, for your generous help with the book cover.

And Sacha! Thanks! I found formatting the table of contents very challenging, but you knew how to help me. God bless you.

"Every good and perfect gift is from above, coming down from the Father of the heavenly lights, who does not change like shifting shadows." James 1:17 (NIV)

"And you shall remember the whole way that the Lord your God has led you..." Deuteronomy 8:2 (ESV)

Introduction

I fall in love easily. When I arrived at Libby C. Booth Elementary School for Kindergarten, it was not long before I picked out Johnny D. as a great husband prospect, trying on his last name..."Dana D." I continued that secret choosing in nearly every grade following Kindergarten. Picking the most handsome or the smartest boy, I dreamed early on. I hoped that one day I would be married and have a family of my own.

I dreamed too of college and maybe law school. I loved academics, and most subjects came easy for me. Having the highest grade-point average in my small high school graduating class, I likely would have gotten a good scholarship to attend University of Nevada at Reno.

But I picked marriage. And I'm not sorry, even though my high school counselor told me I was ruining my life...even though that first husband, a young, battle-scarred Marine, didn't stay for long. (Note ^i)

Marriage is a good thing. It's not what I thought it was when I was five. And though I don't yet know everything about marriage, I know this: the joining together of husband and wife is foundational for civilization. And, amazingly, it is a way to glorify the living God.

God exists. He lives! He is three Persons—Father, Son, and Holy Spirit—in perfect, delighted harmony with each other, existing in one Being. (Note ^ii) Many scriptures indicate that God is One, while other passages indicate more than one viewpoint when he is spoken about or when God is speaking. (For instance, see Romans 3:30. Also, in Genesis chapters 18 and 19, God seems to be in heaven while at the same time visiting Abraham in a tangible form. The prophet, Amos, speaks of that same Genesis story in Amos 4:11.)

Jesus said in John 10:30, "I and the Father are one." In the Hebrew translation of John's gospel, this verse uses the word *echad* for *one*.

This Hebrew word can mean one alone or one in a composite sense. That oneness of God encompassing multiple Persons described in John is the same "*one*," (that same unity in diversity) God refers to when speaking of marriage way back in the beginning of the Bible. In Genesis 2:24, speaking of the bride and the groom, God says,

"Therefore a man shall leave his father and his mother and hold fast to his wife, and they shall become one flesh." Here, again, the word *one* is the Hebrew word *echad.*

The two don't become one person, obviously. At least, in a healthy marriage they do not. Each spouse refrains from absorbing or annulling the other. Individuality is preserved and treasured. Their oneness is that of purpose and plans, of delight and agreement.

God is one Being composed of three Persons. I wonder if, in some sense, the marriage creates a new being composed of two persons.

When I first met Roger McKee, I was struck by his frank brashness. My favorite things about him were his Jesus-focus and his unashamed confidence. Those qualities absolutely captivated me. He loved Jesus, and I did too. I knew that without Jesus, I'd never have made it through the previous year. (Or any year since I was born.)

Jesus was the Unifying Element once Roger and I teamed up. And though we strained almost every possible leash and our eventual covenant, it was enough. God in common is enough; because God invented marriage, and he helped us.

In the following pages, I tell the story of how our oneness seemed destined to failure. At one time I was the sad, lonely, and angry wife-of-Roger.

"In a successful marriage, there is no such thing as one's way. There is only the way of both, only the bumpy, dusty, difficult, but always mutual path." – Phyllis McGinley, Pulitzer Prizewinning American author (Quote origin: *The Province of the Heart* 1966)

Part 1. How to Marry Quickly and Ruin Said Marriage Even Quicker

Chapter 1: Shampoo and Snowflakes

In August, a mutual friend, or acquaintance, "introduced" Roger and me. Allen had told Roger what time I would be working, and he stopped by to meet me. I'd been a checker at a large grocery store in Sparks, Nevada, for about a year. In my mid-twenties, I was 5' 5" tall with medium build and long, brown hair with bangs. I was divorced, the mother of two beautiful little kids. Other guys had invited me to go out with them as they came through my check stand. But I'd made up my mind that I wouldn't go out with anyone who just happened by.

Roger was just the next guy in my grocery checkout line. But as he spoke, he caught my attention. He was not just another conveyor belt customer. Direct and loud, here he came:

"Glory! Hallelujah! Hey, Dana, I'm Roger. Allan said I should come over here and meet you. Would you come to my church on Thursday? We're having a great speaker!" (His southern drawl was cute.)

"Oh, hi. Really? Who is it?"

"Me! Glory! Praise God!" he smiled.

"Ummm... (I think I'm busy.")

I didn't go with him that Thursday. But I'd never met anybody quite so boldly Christian, and I was intrigued. I even went to the dairy section after my shift to buy a quart of kefir. That's what he'd purchased. I'd never heard of it before and wanted to find out what that Roger guy was drinking. (The tasty, thick drink left a white, tangy mustache on my upper lip. I found it good.)

It didn't take long for me to accept a dinner invitation. Roger had recently started working for an industrial laundry company. He asked me if I'd go with him to a classy banquet at the MGM Grand Hotel. It had something to do with his job. Three weeks ahead of the dinner he invited me. So, I put it on the calendar and made babysitting arrangements for that evening, September 29.

Roger came by my check stand nearly every day to get a money order. He collected money from customers on his route but couldn't turn in cash to his employer. So, he made his money order stop into an excuse to see me. His one-minute visits made me laugh. Sometimes I found flowers from Roger or a happy little note on my car. What a treat to find those small surprises when I was so tired!

Getting into my small, brown car with lacey panels on either side of the hood when my night shift ended, the sun just rising, pinking Mount Rose (one of the distant mountains towering above Reno), I'd find that Roger had been thinking of me. Instead of facing a super-sleepy drive home, I smiled and made my way east on Highway 80. Driving the quick thirty miles, I hoped maybe someday somebody would care—somebody besides the kids, Mom, and Annette, who had been my best friend since ninth grade. I began to look forward to seeing Roger.

But he hadn't mentioned a couple of details about our big date, like the time. So, I especially watched for that good-looking guy to come by my work the last week of September. Was I meeting him in town? Monday the 24th came and went. No Roger. The 25th, no Roger. The 26th—28th, still no Roger. We'd not exchanged phone numbers or even last names. I'd have called him. When I left work Saturday morning and he hadn't stopped by to let me know the important particulars, I figured the date was off. I was a little disappointed, but it was not that big a deal.

Working the graveyard shift involved checking out any customers and also putting up light stock like candy and spices. There, in the freezing cold store, I learned to drink coffee. For a quarter, the vending machine gurgled and spit instant coffee into a small foam cup. I drank it for the warmth. And for the aroma, which was far more inviting than the taste. I thought the caffeine was probably a good idea too. But it didn't cure my sleepiness.

Annette (usually I called her *'Net*) watched my kids every work night, and she got them to school and daycare every weekday morning. She was their other mother and always had been. 'Net was as constant as seedtime and harvest. But she was especially dear and present to us that year. I had divorced my straying husband and started working outside my home at a 24-hour grocery store. Plus, I was going to real estate school (an endeavor that never went very far.) After work and a little sleep, I'd go to 'Net's for my kids in the afternoon. Bringing them home, I'd prepare our evening meal.

Annette had agreed to take care of the kids that September evening, but now, I would get to be home with Benji and Ella. 'Net wouldn't need to be on evening duty. After supper, I decided to shampoo my hair in the kitchen sink. Finishing up, I heard somebody knock at the front door.

I wrapped a towel around my hair and answered the door, dripping. There was Roger. His green eyes widened when he saw me and his eyebrows shot up, apparently working out that I wasn't expecting him.

I was not. My thoughts swirled. Really?! Goodness! Roger's here…

With his somewhat unruly mane of black hair and a black mustache; his muscular frame dressed in a tan three-piece suit; his feet shod in shiny, brown, dress shoes, he was way more handsome than in his work uniform. He held a gift of fragrant, long-stemmed pink posies. And there I stood in jeans and pajama top, my hair tucked into a damp towel.

I began explaining that he'd never told me what time to be ready. I hadn't known if he was picking me up, or if I was meeting him in Reno. He defended himself by saying that he had let me know he would be here at this time.

No. I'd have been ready. I wanted to go. I just didn't know…

Suddenly Roger thrust the bouquet at me and asked if he could use the bathroom. While he was in there (praying for grace, he told me later), I called 'Net. Could she still watch the kids? She could.

3

I convinced Roger I could dry my hair and be ready in fifteen minutes if he had time to wait that long. The ride into town was stressful and quieter than I pictured. I had pulled it off. I'd gotten myself together in record time. He commented that I looked nice, and I did feel pretty.

I'd put on my slim floor-length, white, polyester dress with the bunch of rhinestones on the center bodice. Its filmy shoulder wrap and my five-inch, white leather, platform shoes completed the outfit. But I think the problem was that he'd run late, and then I'd made him even later. Time pressure, what a joy killer.

At the dinner I discovered Roger was not going to sit with me. He would be grabbing bites of his meal in hurried snatches here and there because his General Manager had asked him to photograph the event. So, I settled in to do one of my least favorite things, make conversation with total strangers, while Roger's employer explained all the intricacies of the sales contest. The boss interspersed detailed rules with a lot of nodding and pointing, directing Roger to scramble to shoot something with every gesture.

If Roger had taken me straight home afterward, I bet I wouldn't be sitting here looking back over years and years of matrimony with this man. But I'm so glad he rescued the evening by focusing on our date after the dinner was over. He showed me around the glamorous MGM with its soft carpets and crystal chandeliers.

Before the laundry company job, Roger had worked in one of the gourmet kitchens in that brand new hotel casino. The MGM boasted the world's largest casino floor at the time. There were two theaters, various ballrooms, seven restaurants, at least a dozen bars, and even a bowling alley.

Roger bought us two glasses of white wine (my first ever!) and sang me some silly songs as we took the elevator up as far as it would go to look out over the sparkling little basin where Reno sits. What a breathtaking venue and view! Last he took me to meet some of the guys cleaning up in Caruso's, the fancy Italian restaurant, where he introduced me as his wife. Roger was incorrigible.

Roger McKee listens to music whenever he can, almost any kind of music. One type he loves, bluegrass, I wasn't familiar with. But it reminded me of the hymns we sang in a country church in

Pennsylvania where I'd learned to sing parts as a middle-schooler.

I think Roger's music roots, underlying all his other favorites, is instrumental country music. Not long after our MGM date, he took me to a small bar in Harrah's, in downtown Reno, to see Doug Kershaw, a fiddle player he admired. I'd never heard of the Ragin' Cajun, but his energetic, bow-shredding, foot-stomping music impressed me. When we walked outside the casino, big, fluffy snowflakes were falling amid the shimmer and glitz of South Virginia Street's neon lights.

Roger kissed me, and I liked it. We began truly considering marriage right then and there.

"Passion makes every detail important; there is no realism like the insatiable realism of love." – G.K. Chesterton, British writer and philosopher. (Quote from *A Handful of Authors: Essays on Books and Writers*, New York: Sheed and Ward, 1953) Found in The Quotable Chesterton; *A Topical Compilation of the Wit, Wisdom and Satire of G.K. Chesterton* edited by George J. Marlin et. al. Published by IMAGE BOOKS, A Division of Doubleday & Company, Inc. Garden City, New York 1987)

Chapter 2: Laundry Truck Proposal

Roger worked a jillion hours a week at his route sales job with the laundry company. I worked my forty-hour week and took care of my kids. Roger and I didn't get to see one another very often.

The behemoth laundry truck was Roger's usual location. Thus, it was completely logical that he proposed marriage to me in that truck. It happened like this:

One day each week, Roger's route brought him near my house. Early on a chilly, bright November day, he came lumbering up and parked out front. I noticed his big, Red Star truck lurching to a stop under the willow tree, and I ran outside to meet him. Good-looking can't be hidden by a white shirt with a name tag sewn on and navy-blue uniform pants. I still wore my royal blue polyester uniform from the previous night's work. We hugged amid the rails of hanging uniforms, piles of rolled mats, his boom box playing the Christian radio station, KNIS. Roger got down on one knee and asked me if I would marry him.

Instantly and happily, I replied, "Yes!"

We spoke for a few minutes before he had to take off to go about his workday. We agreed. April looked like a good month for a wedding.

Before he brought me a diamond engagement ring on Christmas Eve, the date had been moved. Roger's boss wouldn't give him any time off during April due to the all-important sales push. April was the sales-contest month. So, we changed our wedding day to a Saturday in March.

One way I arranged my life to see Roger more was to take him up on his invitation and leave my church, Life Center. I began attending his. Two years earlier, Roger had moved a few hundred miles from Oregon to come to Reno, helping establish that little assembly.

The Sparks Foursquare Church was a lot smaller than Life Center. Their congregation of ten or twelve met in a single-car garage where the roll-up door was hidden, curtained by a white drape. That backdrop highlighted the small wooden pulpit from which our large Pastor Garth delivered clear biblical sermons. I played piano for them. We sang hymns and contemporary Christian choruses. Each Sunday Benji and Ella were taught their children's church lesson by Garth's friendly wife, Katie, inside the house when the sermon began. We worshiped together and grew closer.

Our plans began in earnest. Should we have a small wedding or something bigger and more traditional? Having never married before, Roger maintained he wanted a church wedding, a fine event with white gown, tuxedoes, and everything. I was easily persuaded to get on board with whatever he wanted.

Well, I wasn't keen on the reception he envisioned with an orchestra, ballroom floor for dancing, China and crystal place settings at a sit-down dinner, etc. Too expensive. He eventually saw the reality of that and agreed to a much simpler reception. But Roger was right. It was a good thing to go out of our way to make a beautiful ceremony and memory.

Pastor Garth would marry us. He set us up with five weeks of premarital counseling which involved an in-depth personality test. We "flunked" an important part of said test. I remember Garth's face. It was serious, even grave. He advised,

"You two need to wait more than the couple months you're planning on. Look at these results. Your anger is off the charts!"

"But I don't feel angry. Well, not all the time."

"If we do get angry with each other, we know how to repent, Right?" We'll say we're "Sorry," and make up.

"We love one another. We both love Jesus. It'll be okay."

How bad could it be, we wondered? Just like TV ads for a sugary cereal, we thought, "We can't get enough" of each other. To avoid falling into sexual sin, we'd keep our wedding plans right where they were. (Note [iii])

Funny how we viewed counsel as a formality. We didn't take much of it to heart.

In the Bible, Job attributed good counsel to the Lord: "With God are wisdom and might; he has counsel and understanding." (Job 12:13).

And King Solomon warned, "Without counsel plans fail, but with many advisers they succeed." (Proverbs 15:22).

Taking heed to counsel is a sign of wisdom, but we weren't paying attention. Trouble loomed if that personality test was right. But we forged ahead.

I did have a secret. My heart was still in pieces over Mr. Babb, Benji and Ella's dad. I'd helped lead him to Jesus, and that guy had been my husband for eight years. If he'd repented of his leaving us, if he'd come back and asked me to, I'd have dropped Mr. McKee in a heartbeat. Not a good detail to leave out of all our wedding planning and counseling.

For a solid year I had cried over being abandoned by him. Maybe longer. This marrying Mr. Right/Mr. Handsome Christian/Mr. I-Did-Not-Lead-You-to-the-Lord was me trying to move on. I was spent. I wanted no more of looking back to figure out just how long it had been since my husband went away. I hated being single. I wished for a father figure for my seven-year-old son and four-year-old daughter. And they loved Roger. He was playful and fun with my kids, so I would try marriage again. It would be good.

But I noticed that Roger did have a few faults. He did not think McDonald's Happy Meals were fit for kids to eat, though I was a pretty big fan. I hadn't run into a Mickey D hater ever before. What a surprise to find that my fiancé was definitely one! (He didn't eat fast food, but he gladly fed us the greasy ninety-nine-cent buffet at Reno's Circus Circus casino. This made me scoff at his ideas for better meal choices.)

Another fault was that Roger had a habit of making up a number. When asked a question that involved time frame, distance, pretty much anything quantifiable, he seemed to say whatever number came to mind. I wouldn't have dreamed of doing that. Being correct about all things was super important to me. This caused issues.

The first big one was over my simple question, "When did you 'get saved'?" I asked this question soon after we met in my check stand with all his loud "Glory, hallelujahs." I really was curious to know how long he had been following the Lord Jesus.

He answered, "About five years."

So, I figured out what year that would have been. I guess Roger didn't think he had to give exact information to me, a woman he'd just met. Actually, I don't know how he rationalized that kind of thing. But when we basically immediately got serious about our relationship, it never occurred to him to revisit that answer of his. Later, I did the math and found that the Mother's Day he was converted was only two and a half years before we met. It wasn't 1974, but probably 1977. So, my Roger was a baby Christian. Yet he was an "elder" in the church?!

So what? Roger was obviously changed. He was no longer a trippy hippy. He'd cut his thick, long, black hair clear up to where it did not touch his shoulders, and he was out to win the world for Jesus, for goodness sake. But I was counting on a mature Christian husband if and when I ever got married again. I felt lied to.

One last fault…We had decided we wouldn't jump into bed together until we were husband and wife. But Roger was pushy in his physical advances. Sometimes when we were alone, he pushed me past excitement and anticipation. I could have worked on speaking up, stating that he was being inappropriate and that I was uncomfortable. (Note iv)

He seemed to know that he was in danger of crossing an important line and did his part to limit our times alone. We kept to our goal, that of holding our union in high honor and keeping our marriage bed undefiled, as instructed in Hebrews 13:4. And we managed; we didn't defile the bed. But we came close. In my opinion, that too was Roger's fault, and I failed to take responsibility.

I was not a quick-on-my-feet, clear communicator. And I could have set a better standard appropriate for a godly woman. I needed words. I needed time but I didn't ask for it.

James 1:5 "If any of you lacks wisdom, let him ask God, who gives generously to all without reproach, and it will be given him."

Chapter 3: Evangelist. "Wah-joe." No Brains.

A bolder evangelist for the gospel you'd never find. Roger headed up a street-witnessing group he named The Force of Righteousness. Preaching and handing out literature in parks and on street corners around Reno, he was working in the Lord's harvest field. His life had been saved and turned around by meeting the Lord Jesus, our Master. So, he naturally wanted to share the Good News with anybody and everybody. Some of the guys who prayed with him in his Force of Righteousness ministry adventures began attending church and became strong in faith.

Most of Roger's witness was to casino workers. Reno has a lot of them: hotel desk clerks, card game dealers, dancers, waiters, kitchen help, security personnel—you name it. Depression statistics are high in "The Biggest Little City in the World." People find out that gambling, going to shows, trying to entertain oneself, and hanging out in the bright lights are all fun for a season, but not forever. People need Jesus. Their heart's home is the God who made them, the Triune God—Father, Son, and Holy Spirit.

Roger was and is tireless in sharing the message that:

"God loves you and sent his one and only Son into the world that you might know him. He is mighty to save you."

Roger and his friend Terry shared a house up in the brown hills west of Reno. The first time I went there to visit Roger, he was just finishing up roasting a turkey. It wasn't a holiday, but the aromas in his house smelled like Thanksgiving. Roger made me a delicious hot turkey sandwich and played one of his favorite radio preacher programs—R. W. Shambach. He had it blaring over the most scratchy, static-filled station imaginable. I was impressed that he could glean spiritual nourishment through that audible snowstorm.

Despite being the busiest man I knew, servicing his laundry route and helping with the church ministries, Roger studied Hermeneutics and Old and New Testament Studies by correspondence. He took these from Life Bible College in the Los Angeles area, thinking God might be calling him to preach regularly sometime in the future. Pastor Garth administered exams in an upstairs office at their house.

I remember meeting Roger there one time, arriving a bit early. Roger was finishing up an exam. Four-year-old Ella stood at the bottom of Garth and Katie's stairs and yelled for "Wah-joe!" "Wah-jooooe, come down hee-ohh!" Very cute! She loved the attention Roger gave her.

Benji loved Roger too. Roger loved to wrestle and play with both of them. He was an expert at making them smile, having been a successful, full-time portrait photographer for four years. Playful at heart, he was genuinely interested in my kids and made allowances for their childish ways.

I think Garth and Katie weren't so sure about us. But I was thrilled.

Besides, I had been married once upon a time, and I thought I'd learned most of the important lessons. Even if Roger didn't, I knew all about this marriage business.

Juxtaposed with self-confidence was uncertainty. I had prayed about my loneliness; I had prayed about becoming Roger's wife. I'd asked if this big step was what the Lord wanted for me. "God, have you sent this man into our lives? Or am I just groping around like usual?"

My little kids were starved for the male companionship of a dad. They were smitten with Roger. But I'd had two other guy friends out to our house for company since their dad had left us. One was a godly, good man. The other, not so much. Now Roger was coming to visit. I didn't want to keep letting my kids get attached to "some guy" and continue to change my mind, jerking them around. The first two men showed up on my radar screen far too soon after my divorce for me to really be free to pursue anything serious. And I don't know if I even understood that it was too soon at the time.

When I prayed about Roger, I had a sense of permission from God. Not of direction. Mom's strong example of never dating anybody after she left Dad—then later, found that he'd divorced her—was important to me. Mom was against remarriage and based that conviction on scripture. For instance, in Luke 16:18 Jesus said, "...he who marries a woman divorced from her husband commits adultery." To Mom's thoughtful, student's mind, the Bible taught that any remarriage is sinful while the ex-mate lives.

But looking further, taking other scriptures into consideration, the Bible indicates two legitimate reasons for divorce: adultery and abandonment. Though divorce is terrible and shouldn't be our choice, there are circumstances in which divorce is appropriate.

No divorce is the rule; adultery and abandonment are exceptions to the rule. (See Matthew 5:32, and Matthew 19:9 on adultery as a scriptural exception regarding divorce. Also see 1 Corinthians 7:15 which speaks to abandonment as scriptural grounds. (Note [v]) I was a victim of both those exceptions.

Divorce means the marriage is over. Unmarried adults can marry. Unmarried Christian adults can marry "in the Lord." (1 Corinthians 7:1-16)

I believed then, and I'm convinced now, that the Lord honors our paperwork. (Note [vi])

Regarding God's leading for choosing a mate, Roger said he knew I was the one when he noticed where I placed the bouquet of pink flowers he bought me on that first big date. He explained all this to me much later.

Months before he met me, when he'd given flowers to a woman, he asked the Lord for a sign. If she was "the one," she would set the flowers on her dining room table. I think this test of his went through more than one woman. The flowers were always placed somewhere else. And he forgot about it.

But when Roger showed up at my house for dinner a couple of weeks after he'd given me the bouquet gift, he saw the vase of flowers on my table! They were drooping and withered, but they were still there.

12

I apologized and cleared them away before our meal, throwing them in the trash. But he remembered. It was Roger's sign — a word from the Lord to him.

From our second date on I was pretty sure that Roger was going to be my Mr. Right. So, I had him out to the house for dinner whenever possible. It struck me that cow brains would be a good entree possibility. Mom had fed them to us children when I was little, and I liked them. She had read up on all kinds of things that would make kids smarter, and she tried everything. Anyway, she sold us kids on eating them, and she fixed them often when I was five or six.

I had not fried beef brains in years, and Benji and Ella had never tasted them. But one of the times Roger came to our house for dinner I decided to go gourmet. I'd serve brains. It was a bit of a tedious process to peel the membrane off, cut it up, dredge the pieces in egg wash and cracker crumbs, season them just right, and fry them to perfection. The steaming, browned nuggets looked and smelled good.

I couldn't wait to taste them again and thought I would just surprise him. Roger was surprised, all right. He was looking forward to the meal, but when he bit down, and the texture was all wrong, way too soft, he let out a disgusted holler! Let's just say, Husband #1 and Husband #2 were going to have this one thing completely in common. No brains for dinner.

"My most brilliant achievement was my ability to be able to persuade my wife to marry me." — Winston Churchill, Soldier, Best-Selling Author, Journalist, Twice Prime Minister of UK (Quote found at Reader's Digest online, rd.com Also found at brainyquote.com, accessed 04-25-2022)

Chapter 4: My Hero!

Marrying Roger after knowing him six months...I knew it was a "jump into life" deal. At age twenty-seven, I risked more in some ways than the first time. There were many more variables. Marriage at age seventeen involved only the two of us. And though we each had our baggage in that early marriage, we had nearly two years together as husband and wife before Benjamin was born. When Roger and I married, we started with four of us, and within a month, we were five! Baby #3 was a wonderful surprise, but definitely a surprise.

But I have skipped over something pretty important: we got married!

Finding that Pastor Garth was licensed to officiate at nuptials only in California, we looked for a venue across the Nevada-California border. We found a pretty church building in the picturesque town of Truckee.

The wedding morning dawned sunny and beautiful. I wore a feminine white wedding gown with a lace empire bodice and organza layered long skirt, ruffled at the bottom. My bouquet bloomed with daisies and yellow roses. The guys wore white tuxes trimmed in brown. My dear friend, Annette, was my Matron of Honor. She and Ella wore light lemon-yellow dresses that 'Net and I had made. Ella was our flower girl, Benji was our ring-bearer, and Roger's friend, Jimmy, was Best Man.

I'd planned to wear my hair down for the wedding. I knew a way to fix an updo, but I had recently gotten my hair cut in long layers at a salon, something of a big splurge for me. I always had just worn my hair long. But with it shorter and different than usual, I couldn't style it the way I knew.

Roger's last-minute request was to have it up. I never thought about going back to a beauty shop to have it done, nor did I explain to him my thoughts about his request. He'd have let me do what I wanted, I bet. I just twisted my hair up, stuck in some pins to hold it there, and fastened on my veil.

Heart racing a little, I got ready in the chapel's spacious ladies' room. As I pointed out before, I had noticed a couple of faults in my soon-to-be husband. But, at this point, I knew the Lord was calling Roger and me to married life together. I applied my make-up, talked to 'Net, helped Ella into her pretty dress, and set out to start a new chapter— to be a bride!

My Grandma Alice had made it out to our ten o'clock A. M. wedding up in the mountains. Of course, Mom, my always faithful and honest cheerleader was there. My cousins and our friends from church had taken their seats in the Chapel of the Pines.

Then I offended in a way I didn't anticipate; it had to do with a mint. As I was about to take my brother Cliff's arm for him to hold me down to earth so I wouldn't float but walk up the aisle, I put a fruity-flavored Cert into my mouth. There stood my groom, my Roger, at the front of the church looking nervous but so handsome. I wanted to make sure I would have good breath for this lovely thing that was unfolding, this very day!

Morning light streamed through the blue stained-glass window where a white dove shone. Irregular, brown stonework covered the front of the building and surrounded the resplendent window. The sharp, fresh scent of Sugar Pines and the butterscotchy-vanilla aroma of Jeffrey Pines wafted in through the doors. I loved this perfect setting. My sleepy kids and 'Net and Jimmy and Pastor Garth were ready! This breezy, bright morning in this ideal place would seal our forever love.

But Roger seemed distracted. As I walked - happy, excited, and confident toward him - I didn't even think about the fact that I was spoiling my smile with that little mint. I now know that he was thinking like a photographer, but at the time, his critical frown and first remark to me at the front—"What do you have in your mouth?!"—was not what I expected.

I asked him to repeat himself. He said it again. I had understood him correctly. No compliment. No excitement about this beautiful ceremony…Nothing about tonight?!

His question hurt my feelings.

Looking at the portraits, I later saw he had a valid point. (Note [vii]) But at the time, it knocked the wind out of me. I thought for a second that I should turn and run out the church door, right out into the woods.

I didn't run. We made it. I stayed for our self-written vows. I truly wish I had a copy of those now, but I don't. I know that I didn't agree to obey or submit. Roger had agreed with me that we'd promise to "submit to each other." I don't think we used any part of the traditional vows that include the beautiful promise to "cherish."

A friend sang "Morning Has Broken." Pastor Garth did the ceremony. We repeated the vows (such as they were) and gave each other rings. The Dana Babb/Roger McKee wedding was glorious, if a little stressful, and it did hold us together through many perilous times ahead. Barely.

Before the wedding, on a trip from Reno to Truckee, taking care of some rehearsal dinner details, a terrifying, nightmarish escape or suicide attempt unfolded in a car next to us. As their car passed ours, a woman opened the passenger door and seemed to be trying to jump out of the speeding vehicle. The man driving was holding onto her hair! A few minutes later we saw the same car on the side of the highway. Roger pulled over too, jumped out, and ran toward the other car. He stopped short of that car and began yelling, "Let her go!"

Whatever the altercation, it continued. Roger started throwing rocks at the car and kept shouting. I was frightened for Roger's safety and maybe for me and the kids too; what if the guy in that car had a weapon? Unbelievably the guy burst out of the car, running toward us! Roger dashed back, got in, and quickly pulled out of the small rest area. The woman got the guy locked out of her car when he came toward Roger. She got herself into the driver's seat and peeled out just behind us. We slowed as she drove by, lowering her window a little bit. Shakily but clearly she repeated, "Thank you; you saved my life."

Just up the road at Boomtown, Roger called the police to report the incident and to describe the guy who was now hitchhiking. I saw a heroic side of my Roger that day that the kids and I will never forget.

"There is no more lovely, friendly, and charming relationship, communion, or company than a good marriage." – Martin Luther, German Reformer of the Protestant Reformation, Bible translator, and author

Chapter 5: Honeymooning

Our reception was a small gathering featuring cake and punch with dear friends and family at Terry's house (formerly Roger's place too). A sweet woman from church made and decorated a beautiful wedding cake for us. Its three perfect tiers and cream cheese frosting made up the most delicious carrot cake ever!

After we opened thoughtful gifts, lovingly given, Roger and I jumped into my car to head off on our honeymoon. That's when I found out we were simply going to grab a motel along the way. With all the planning and preparations for the wedding, I'd assumed that Roger had arranged for a nice hotel for our wedding night. He hadn't.

We stopped at a not great, not terrible place in Susanville. "Mediocre" would be a fair description. With cigarette-smoke-smelling, red, velvet draperies.

Expectations can be a trap. Most couples have found this out at some point. With Roger's reaction to my mint as strike one and the dumpy motel as strike two, things weren't looking good for our one-day-old marriage. I was let down and a little worried. And when I let my groom know that I was unhappy, he became frustrated and unhappy too. It had bothered me that Roger let himself be bothered by something minor—the Cert. Now he was bothered that I was bothered.

Roger wasn't at all like the husband I knew before. Being the opposite of Mr. Babb was, in many ways, a good thing. That was part of the attraction. But one aspect of my new husband came as a shock. I was unused to being so close to a fiery personality who would throw whatever criticism I dished out right back at me.

My three brothers are distinct, very different individuals. I knew this. I understood that men aren't all the same. Why I thought being married again would be anything like my previous experience, I don't know. Clueless. Contrast my viewpoint with Roger's: I guarantee you; he wasn't worried about the Cert thing for longer than two minutes. Nor did he give a care about how the room was decorated.

It isn't unusual for newlyweds to have difficulties on their honeymoon, so we were normal. I guess.

Not that we did not have fun; we did. Our honeymoon was a four-day drive up the Oregon coast and another couple days in Sacramento. We admired the beauty of God's great creation in the Northwest. We stopped to take photographs of a snow-capped mountain peak, of waves crashing against jagged black rocks, of dainty purple wildflowers, and of each other. We listened to a dozen sermons by one of Roger's favorite radio preachers at the time, playing them on the cassette player in my little brown Corolla. I'd never heard of Kenneth Copeland, but I enjoyed his down-to-earth way of talking. We discovered later that much of his stuff is questionable, teaching that suffering is never God's plan for Christians.

But one point he made that stayed with me is the directional illustration he used regarding faith. It went something like this:

If you are in sin and (ungodly) fear (Note [viii]), going along sad or angry or defeated, when it dawns on you, by the grace of God you repent. (Note [ix]) You realize your mistake, and you turn from your sin, repenting of your failure to trust God. He forgives and enables an about-face. You are immediately rescued from walking in sinful fear, and you're now walking in faith. It's just as if you were walking south, but you turn around. Immediately you're walking north.

We drove and talked; we stopped at some great seafood restaurants. When Roger took me to Corvallis to introduce me to some friends of his, this quickly turned into something less than fun for me. He unintentionally shut me out of the conversation. Not great. But much of the trip was enjoyable. I'd never been to the wild, rocky coast above California. It was good to settle down and be together.

We found a pretty room overlooking the ocean and stayed there two nights. That hotel had a deserted, secluded beach. The windy shore edged blue-gray, white-capped water.

It was too cold to swim, but we sipped wine and found it was a perfect spot for snuggling in Roger's big, warm, wool cape—a soft, black burnous—he'd bought when traveling in Africa.

When back home, we got the kids from 'Net, loaded them up and took them to Sacramento. There we visited the zoo and treated them to a movie, Disney's "Lady and the Tramp." We stayed overnight, including them in our honeymoon week.

It was a whole month later we got pregnant. I don't remember the details of early indications, pregnancy tests, etc. I never have had morning sickness, so my symptoms were minor. I know I was happy. Ella would be six by the time the baby came, and Benji would be eight and a half. I was glad this new little one was there growing inside me, glad the space between siblings wouldn't be any greater.

In June, after I'd known about the baby for a month, we got to go to "Jesus California Style" in Sacramento. I had never been to a days-long Christian music festival, and I was excited. The kids and I went early with some acquaintances from church. Roger followed, flying down after he finished his workweek. We were camping out. I loved the music and the speakers, but little Benji was sick with asthma.

It was hot, and there was straw everywhere in the camping area. Neither the heat nor the straw and its accompanying molds were good for my poor boy. The heat was getting to me too. Though I wasn't far along in my pregnancy, the summery weather in Sacramento was uncomfortable. Humidity made it feel far hotter than the dry heat in Fernley, our little Nevada town.

Roger and I got to meet some interesting Christian people. One outstanding couple we enjoyed getting to know was Mr. and Mrs. Charles McPheeters. Charlie and Judy headed up a street ministry in Hollywood called the Holy Ghost Repair Service. There they ministered to the same down-and-outer type folks Roger had preached to on the streets of Reno with his Force of Righteousness. Roger and Charlie shared anecdotes, prayer requests, and encouragement.

We heard James Robison preach, Mike Warnke do his comedy show, and Reba Rambo sing. It was encouraging and uplifting to be there.

Yet, heading home from the Jesus festival I somehow ended up in the very back of a van, stuffed in with the kids and the sleeping bags and smelly, dirty clothes. Roger was in the front with other adults. It made me mad that he allowed the seating to be arranged that way, but I thought I'd at least be able to get out and stretch. And I did want some ice cream.

"Let's stop for ice cream!" I yelled.

"No." Roger replied, "We're not stopping."

I was not a happy camper.

When we first met, Roger took care of his responsibilities at his work and ministry as his priority, and I admired that about him. Though I could see he liked me a lot right away, he didn't make it out to my place to have dinner with us very often. I felt that showed steadiness and self-control. He didn't idolize me.

But when I was relegated to the back of that van with the kids and the tire iron and the tarps and tent pegs that hot June evening, and Roger would not sit near me or be appealed to for an ice cream stop, I wished for a little bit of idolizing. Or just respect.

"In marriage, being the right person is as important as finding the right person." – Wilbert Donald Gough, American Preacher and Bible student

Chapter 6: First Move

It turns out, Roger was following bad advice. Pastor Garth was telling him that a husband's leadership role involves laying down the law. The wife needs to submit. No time like the present to put the wife in her place. Garth learned better in about five years, and he and Katie benefited. But at the time, I don't think they were doing very well. And I know that we were suddenly not doing well. Garth's bad counsel in the months after our marriage didn't help us at all.

I was getting a little scared of my husband. Instead of the happy "Glory to God! Hallelujah!" smiling, interested man, he seemed distant. Down. And I guessed he was uncertain about me as well. I became a day-to-day mom and wife who could be grumpy and unforgiving. I was becoming less an admirer of my Roger.

After we married, Roger initially moved in with me and the kids. My home was a single-story, white rancher with yellow shutters, its front garden boasting flower beds and a graceful willow. There was a cute, short fence made of rough-hewn boards edging the front lawn where the willow's lady-like tresses brushed the grass when we forgot to trim her for a few months. Our back lawn was a terrific place to lie on one's back and admire the Milky Way. There I taught Benji and Ella to identify Orion and the Big Dipper. In the daytime the kids could play on a platform and monkey bars that stood between the lawn and a farmer's field.

But there were too many memories in that place for me. I'd bought it with my first husband and lived there through our breakup. So, I was anxious to have a new start in a different home. I rented out the house, and we moved to one in Sparks, Nevada, next door to the building where our growing church had just moved. This house made our family much closer, not only to our fellowship, but to both our workplaces. So, though it meant a new elementary school for Benji and Ella, it was good to relocate there.

I guess moves always take more resources and gumption than you think. I was working at the store every weekday, my body was building a baby, (which takes a lot of energy), and I was not unpacking very quickly.

Roger's routes always made long, tiring workdays for him. But, despite that, coming home from work one day I found that he'd beat me home, worked on unpacking, and had it nearly all finished. Boxes were stacked outside. I walked inside to see how nicely he'd arranged everything! How my husband blessed his tired wife that day!

In the Sparks house, Benji quietly hunted for a passage to Narnia. For a seven-year-old, Benji was a great reader. He'd consumed all seven *Chronicles of Narnia* more than once. He was convinced that he would find his way into C. S. Lewis' imaginary land in the six- by-eight-foot weed garden behind the house.

Benji was a talkative little boy, but he did not talk a lot about this. It was serious. I knew he dreamed about the Lion, Aslan, the Pevensie kids, and all the characters, because he told me his dreams in detail. Maybe the make-believe land of talking animals, even though threatened by wicked forces, was safer than the reality of the new school situation, the new "Roger" situation, the chaos of our busy schedules, and the lostness he and Ella felt when Roger and I argued.

Our friend, Jimmy-the-Best-Man, needed a place to stay, so he moved in and slept on our couch. I remember trying repeatedly to get Jimmy to hang his towel straight in our only bathroom…

Plus, I remember him goofing around with Benji. In the horseplay a light fixture got broken. My son panicked over the shattered glass shade, but Jimmy assured him it was okay.

"Roger won't be mad."

Benji whispered, "Not Roger…my mom!"

Then Jimmy got scared. "Shh! Oh no!"

I can picture his wide blue eyes!

"Marriage is like twirling a baton, turning handsprings, or eating with chopsticks. It looks easy until you try it." – Helen Rowland, American journalist and humorist

Two favorite Bible verses on love:

"There is no fear in love, but perfect love casts out fear..." 1 John 4:18

"Let love be genuine. Abhor what is evil; hold fast to what is good." Romans 12:9

Chapter 7: A Wilderness of Trouble

I wasn't always somebody who caused fear and trembling at the mere thought of my displeasure. I was born weighing just under seven pounds, Dana E. Grim, to J.R. Grim, who was in his late forties, and Audrey H. Grim, nearly twenty. I came into the world in eastern Nevada, USA. My dad had two sons by his first marriage. And Mom and Dad had become the proud parents of my brother, Ray, a year before me. So, I was the first girl.

They were pretty happy about me, I think. Mom called me *Sugar*, and Daddy called me his *Little Flower*. They went on to give me two more brothers and a sister in the next few years. Douglas was a year younger than me. The little kids were Carol and Cliffy. We moved to California when I was two or three. Dad preached there in the tiny town of Portola. After that, he continued to refer to himself as a preacher, but he never later ministered to a congregation, that I knew of. Except our family. He did preach to us.

A favorite memory in the Portola house includes toads under the kitchen sink. My vantage point was behind Ray and Douglas, peeking over their shoulders at the spotted, brown, big-eyed creatures. Ray and Douglas could poke the toads to make them hop.

I have memories too of Mom teaching Sunday School in that little fellowship. She had my brothers and me memorize nursery rhymes and passages of scripture: Psalm 1 and Psalm 23, Romans 5:1 and 5:8 are some I still remember. She knew so many songs and great Bible stories! Mom was amazing. And we got to have her home with us kids while Daddy worked for the first seven or eight years of my life.

A medley of Sunday School songs I remember from that era started with one called,

The Lord Knows the Way Through the Wilderness by Sidney E. Cox

"The Lord knows the way through the wilderness,

"And all I have to do is to fahh-low,

"The Lord knows the way through the wilderness,

"And all I have to do is to fahh-low.

"Strength for today is mine alway -

"So why should I worry about to-mahh-row?

"The Lord knows the way through the wilderness,

"And all I have to do is to follow."

Capitol CMG Publishing, License # 1018904. Copies purchased 09/09/21.

Wilderness times were ahead, but God truly was there always leading, when I was little and when I was grown. Not that I followed perfectly. No matter. He comes after his lost ones.

My children, Benji and Ella, were great little kids, but sometimes they needed correction. Roger and I got into most of our big hassles over how to do that, how to guide them. I realized it was a parent problem, not just a puzzle for stepparents. I tried to explain that to Roger, but my words didn't help.

I'd never had the kids call Roger *Dad.* (Though they did begin calling him *Dad* as adults.) Benji and Ella had a dad. I wanted them to know they were conceived in a home that had been a loving place. Later I wondered if that was the best idea, but that was my thought process at the time. So, they called Roger by his name. I think that bothered him. He may have felt the first-name basis implied disrespect. I don't know. Roger told me he had called his dad worse.

Old Fool was one bad name he used to refer to his dad. Roger was not taught to respect his father, or say, "I love you," to either his dad or mom. Nor does he remember being told those three, simple, loving words when he was a child. His home became a volatile, frightening place after his dad stopped working regularly.

Fearless little Roger, an only child, stayed out of the way as much as possible. He played at making forts in the woods near his South Carolina home. Only two things scared him: his mom slinging frying pans around when his father came home, and his dad roaring and crashing into furniture. Dorothy and Clark separated for a while when Roger was seven years old; divorce happened when he was thirteen.

Roger was providing for my kids and loving them. He'd sold his new motorcycle when I met him, getting rid of it before we married to avoid the payments causing excessive strain on our budget. In a hundred ways Roger was the day-to-day dad Benji and Ella needed. But suddenly, Roger made an impulsive, bad decision.

I'd just finished telling the kids not to do some unremembered thing. Roger contradicted me and told them to disobey me and do whatever it was. They obeyed me, not him. It was uncomfortable and confusing, and not a victory for me. These two dear kids and I had grown up together in a sense. Roger should have known to tread a little more lightly as he took over the big job of fathering them. But his was on-the-job training...

Our home was becoming a stressful place, but not wanting to give up, I prayed,

"Lord, help Roger get a clue! And help me get my attitude figured out."

I wanted to know how to love and respect my husband. I wanted him to realize how much the kids did like and admire him. After praying, I'd feel calmed and reassured.

But then Roger came home. And the temporary quiet left when he entered. Yelling and sometimes pushing ensued. He never hurt me, but the tension in our house reminded me of the way I had to tiptoe around my dad. I did not want that uncertain environment for my kids. Could Roger and I fix this? Could we have peace at home?

Five months pregnant, I found it hard to be on my feet working eight hours a day. I was looking forward to quitting and staying home for the latter part of my pregnancy. Just to be home, to cook and take care of the house and the kids and see if I could figure out my new husband...that was what I wanted so much.

Roger and I had discussed my quitting, and now the time drew near. I gave my two-week notice at the store. That last day of work we fought again. I have no idea what the details of the disagreement were except that it was about the kids. As Roger dropped me off at work, I remember his angry expression, his gestured emphasis, and his words. "You'd better keep that job."

But my boss had already hired a woman to take my place.

The Psalms have been a great comfort to me. Here are a couple references where the psalmists model prayers for anyone in trouble:

"Save me, O God! For the waters have come up to my neck." Psalm 69:1

"You who have made me see many troubles and calamities will revive me again; from the depths of the earth you will bring me up again." Psalm 71:2

Chapter 8: Separation

I went inside the store. For a few minutes I didn't know what to do. Then I realized I had to take Roger's veiled threat seriously. Going to my boss, I asked if I could continue to work. I told him the situation. I didn't think I was going to stay married to Roger. He graciously agreed to let me continue working five hours a day. I was devastated and angry, but grateful to have a job.

In the next few days, I talked to Mom about the kids and me staying in her furnished, unoccupied mobile home back out in Fernley. She said we could. So, I prepared to move. I didn't tell Roger but packed up while he was at work. It was too hard to be married.

It is difficult to be married, but where does one go to sign up for the easy life? The trouble-free life is not on God's "good and perfect gift" list. The challenging events he allows to come to me, he alone knows how to work together with all the other easier-looking events for my good if I love and trust him. And even when I temporarily don't trust, he is at work. (Remember Romans 8:28.)

When I left Roger, I changed the way I took checks at work. Thirty or forty times a day I put my initial and last name on the back of each one. I decided that the McKee name just didn't "take." I'd been Dana Babb for nearly ten years; I'd go back to making my name match my two kids who were born. I went to the office, talked to Alice, the bookkeeper, and told her I was no longer "D. McKee." I was back to being "D. Babb" on my checks. She said, "Fine."

I worried and grieved about having a third child with no dad. That was sad. But it couldn't be helped. The truly wrenching thing about Roger and me separating, calling it quits, was that we were both Christians. No infidelity had come between us. We should resemble Jesus our Lord who always was in complete agreement with the Father. God's book, the Bible, teaches that marriage reflects a beautiful, heavenly reality. This oneness between husband and wife is special and pure, and in some mysterious way pictures the delight and agreement of the Lord Jesus with the church, the assembly of believers. (See Ephesians 5:21-33, especially verses 31-32.)

Would God leave us, his own people? God promised he wouldn't in Deuteronomy 31:6-8 and Hebrews 13:5. The Lord calls his relationship with his people a marriage. He is our Groom. We are, corporately, his bride. In that holy unity between God and us, there will never be a parting. He is never leaving.

But I was leaving.

Still, I was torn. I felt that not only was I letting down myself and my kids by not staying married, not figuring out how to make Roger's and my relationship good and peaceful, but I was also letting down God's universal church. And society. I felt the burden of discovering that I wasn't a faithful person. I had promised to stay married to Roger "till death do us part" just a few months earlier. But I couldn't go on.

That thirty-mile-one-way commute loomed again too. We had sold my Toyota Corolla and bought a used Audi. When we got it, I thought it would be great to have a luxury car. But the excitement soon fizzled. The Audi was such a junker. Of its many problems, the worst was the way it went through alternators. I changed that expensive device at least three times. The kids and I, out in the middle of nowhere in the desert, would see the headlights dimming...Oh no! Climbing out of our dark, dead car, we'd find ourselves stranded once again!

By the grace of God, I was able to trade the Audi in on a new VW Rabbit. When I first walked into the dealership showroom, I was drawn to a small, white car with blue racing stripes. The salesman tried steering me away, glibly directing me toward a more expensive car, saying,

"You don't want this car. This is the stripped-down model—no carpet, no radio..."

I looked at other cars, considering those with more options before I told the salesman that the stripped-down car was for me. I didn't need carpet and a radio on my loan payments. I just wanted to reliably get from point A to point B. What a relief to find that I could buy a car on my own. I'd been ready to give up on finding anything affordable and good in Reno, but this was it. The Lord provided that little white Rabbit for me.

Though I didn't know it, the Lord was providing something else too, a strong and steady husband. Before I left him, Roger was so appallingly wishy-washy that when we had an argument, he often said we should divorce. Now, developing courage and perseverance, he decided to love me no matter what. That was a big miracle. God alone can change someone as much as Roger changed.

Too bad I didn't care anymore. Hope had died, and my cold heart was frozen toward my husband. I was not doing the *Love Must be Tough* strategy where the hoped-for result is that the offending partner will wise up, and the one who left can come back to the relationship. That was Dr. James Dobson's book. But Roger was just too late. I was taking a page out of a different volume, Margaret Mitchell's *Gone With the Wind*. I agreed with Rhett where he states, "Frankly, my dear, I don't give a doggone, flying leap." Something like that.

"The most difficult years of marriage are those following the wedding." – Gary Smalley, American family counselor and author

Chapter 9: Real Husbands. Lies.

My former husband moved back to Nevada from Texas. He had gone there for about a year, taking the woman he'd run away with. They had married, but now separated from her, he was back in town. The kids were very glad to visit with their daddy. They hadn't seen him regularly since he left us. The timing made it appear that I'd left Roger for Mr. Babb. It's not what happened. But we did fall back into relationship very quickly. I was thrilled, thinking this was the wonderful resolution to my Roger problem.

"My second marriage was just a short-lived, terrible error."

"People make mistakes."

"My 'real husband' is back!"

Mr. Babb seemed to be his former self, not the drug-inhabited, devil-may-care guy he'd suddenly become just before he left us. He began to come around where we were staying. He said all the right things, just what I'd longed for him to say. He was sorry. He loved me and the kids. He'd made an awful blunder in leaving. We talked long hours, and he shared the lessons he had learned in his wanderings. It all sounded true. Perfect.

I visited an attorney and asked if there was a way to get my marriage to Roger annulled. I wished to make the wedding promise like it never happened. The attorney glanced at my obviously pregnant belly and countered, "No, probably not." But he would be happy to help me get a divorce. I began the process.

Roger moved out of our rented Sparks house and got a small apartment in Verdi, Nevada. He began buying me things I'd need for the baby. I had no crib, no diapers, no car seat. Now that car seats were required by law for babies, I'd have to have one of those too.

So, I needed the things Roger brought, and I accepted them. But he'd also bring flowers. I told him,

"Don't waste money on flowers."

"You're too late; I don't like you anymore."

Sometimes Roger would come by my store to talk to me. As soon as I saw him, I asked the manager to have him escorted out.

The Lord had gotten Roger's attention, had installed some tempered steel into his backbone. But God didn't completely tame the southern boy. Roger told me after we reconciled how mightily he struggled against his temptations. Destruction of property tantalized and nearly bewitched him. He pictured himself running over Mr. Babb's brown Yamaha XS11 motorcycle where he saw it parked. Roger had sold his beautiful, metallic blue Yamaha, also an XS11, for us. I'm sure his truck could have made a grease spot of the pretty bike.

Also, the provocation to murder was strong. Envisioning a knife gripped in his hand, Roger wondered if he would be able to stand against it. The taunting of jealousy is described in Proverbs 27:4, "Wrath is cruel, anger is overwhelming, but who can stand before jealousy?"

One time when Mr. Babb and I, embracing, talked beside his motorcycle, Roger interrupted us. His laundry truck slid to a stop in a cloud of dust. Roger jumped out, denounced Mr. Babb, threw back his head, balled up his fists, and laughed a wild cackle!

I just shook my head, embarrassed. It didn't occur to me the danger that had just passed for all three of us. Four, really. Lucas was there, beneath my heart, trusting me. That was a turning point for Roger. He had conquered the snarling demons of wrath, jealousy, and revenge. (Note [x])

The Babb family reunification effort lasted only about four weeks. In that brief time, we talked of re-marrying after the baby was born. It didn't feel like adultery to be with him. He was my "real husband." How could this be wrong?

But I knew that God's word, the Bible, forbade this alternating back to a former husband. In Deuteronomy 24:4 God calls this practice "detestable" or "an abomination" depending on which version you read. But I was contemplating it.

The double sin of remarriage to one's former husband and the presumption it would have involved...it all turned out to be a non-issue. Mr. Babb began to miss his wife and disappeared from my life once again. Forever. I was a wreck.

Roger still pursued me, bringing big and small gifts for the baby. I was sure I could never care for him again. But I no longer hated him. Maybe that was progress.

But I fumed. Angry, I judged God's wisdom and his design for marriage. Nearly gnashing my teeth, I yelled at my Father in heaven, "What are you doing, God?! Why did you dream up the taking of a spouse? I think it's a trick. You created men and women too different from each other. We're too dissimilar to ever successfully work this thing called *marriage*."

Then I remembered that in heaven there will be no marriage. (Matthew 22:29-30.) In the resurrection I wouldn't be wife to either one. Hallelujah! That made me celebrate. But, I thought,

"In the here and now, I am female. I am a wife. There is an incompleteness about being just a wife, just a mom, with no husband, no dad in the home." (Note [xi])

Proverbs 27:8 points out the sad simile: "Like a bird that strays from its nest is a man who strays from his home."

The man of the house, both of them, had left. I felt defenseless and desolate.

But I'm so glad my Father in heaven could take it when I told him what I thought. In no uncertain terms. Even when my thinking was pretty scrambled, he wanted the conversation. Even when it was a one-sided tirade, and not the talking and listening I should have taken time for, my Dad in heaven did not give up on me.

Sticks and stones are hard on bones, Aimed with angry art. Words can sting like anything, But silence breaks the heart. – Phyllis McGinley, American author (Quote found at wonderfulquote.com, accessed 04-25-2022)

Psalm 29:11 "May the LORD give strength to his people! May the LORD bless his people with peace!

Chapter 10: Fire!

My brand-new car caught on fire. It had 3,600 miles on it the day the brakes failed. As I approached a red light on Oddie Boulevard, smoke poured out from under the hood!

It so happened that Mr. Babb was in the car with me when the brakes overheated. I knew by then that he and I were not getting back together. He was too goofed up for words, and he was back on whatever drug had him in its clutches off and on. But he was sick that day, and I'd taken him to the doctor. (I don't remember why his wife didn't help him.) He was in the passenger seat and was the one who pulled up on the emergency brake, stopping the car. Thus, I avoided the looming crash. When he opened the hood, flames leaped up...higher than the roof of my car! A passing motorist had a fire extinguisher.

Afraid of that little car, I wanted the dealer to give me a different one. But Volkswagen of America told me that was not my decision; they would let me know if they'd fix or replace the car. Weighing both options, the adjuster's choice was to fix it. Over the course of the next few months, the dealer loaned me other cars—some not good on mileage, some undependable junkers—while they took their merry time. It ended up being three months!

I found myself resenting that motorist with preparedness tendencies and his ready fire extinguisher! If my car had burned just a bit longer... At the same time, I was beginning to trust again that God knew all, and he was allowing this one more thing on top of all the other trials.

(By the way, the Rabbit lasted until Ben was in high school, Baby #5 came, and we decided our crew was just too big to fit into the little hatchback.)

The desperation that drives women to abort their babies weighed on me early in my pregnancy, when the Roger-Dana duo wasn't doing at all well...that was the first time. If I'd been less convinced that human life begins at conception, I might have considered ending my pregnancy.

And months later when Roger was an annoying stranger and Mr. Babb had just dumped me again, I came close to understanding the despair that pushes women toward abortion. I could never have done it. But I understand the overwhelming uncertainty that can accompany pregnancy. (Note [xii])

Anyone who knows our tall, dark and handsome, strong, smart and loving, grown-up son can immediately see that he was and is worth whatever extra trouble I experienced early in our marriage due to being pregnant. He is one of my greatest blessings. Lucas is a great son, brother to five, caring husband and father, encourager of many, entertainer with hilarity, friend who demonstrates generosity. Aborting him would have been a terrible tragedy.

One thing I greatly missed in the couple of months I'd driven the Rabbit, was a radio. Roger knew that. When the VW people were finally getting close to finishing all the repairs, Roger paid to have a nice radio installed in my car. For my birthday! It was so sweet of him. I still didn't like him, but I did like that Grundig radio.

He came up with another present for that birthday that was so perfect, it was amazing! (Roger is the most thoughtful gift-giver God ever created.)

There's a hill called Painted Rock near the Truckee River that is just beautiful. When the rock was cut to make room for Highway 80, pink, purple, and yellow minerals were exposed in the grays and browns of background rock. Heading toward Fernley from Reno, the freeway wends between a curve of the blue Truckee River on the right and the colorful hill on the left. That scenic view is rare and refreshing desert beauty. Roger photographed it one day and had that work of love and art professionally printed and framed for me.

Chapter 11: Good Counsel

In the midst of my sorrow, anger, and despair, Roger rescued me. He paid for me to see a counselor. I hated to receive this handout from him, but I had to have help, or I was going to totally lose it. Bill-the-Christian-Counselor had a good reputation, so I picked him. I walked into that first appointment and thought the nice-looking, dark-haired counselor seemed professional. But when I sat down and he seated himself behind his sleek office desk, I began the interview by expressing my certainty that he wouldn't be able to extricate me from my dilemma.

I wanted help. I wanted biblical counsel. I wished to obey God's Word, knowing the Bible was the only reliable standard for life and behavior. But I didn't see a way to satisfy what God wanted from me. I didn't have biblical grounds for divorce, but I'd found my new husband so volatile and unpredictable...I'd tried living with him for months. It only got more difficult.

I stated, "I know what the Bible says. But I cannot go back to him."

Bill D. assured me that he was a Christian and he trusted the Bible. But he pointed out my conviction that "I know what the Bible says"...that might be a somewhat arrogant stance.

The counselor asked if I felt I knew everything the Word of God taught.

"Well, if you put it like that..."

I agreed that it did sound inaccurate and prideful.

He offered help if I'd listen and if I'd dare to hope that he might have some light to shed on my situation, some missed insight. At that point, Bill D. backed up and asked me my name.

"Dana Babb. Well, legally, my name is Dana McKee, but I'm going to have that taken care of."

When he asked how I was going to take care of my name, I told him about the lawyer…how I'd been hoping to avoid another divorce. I desired erasure of the marriage to Roger McKee. I told him that the lawyer had even dropped his price.

Bill D. changed the subject and stated that there was something vulnerable about me that made him want to protect me as well. He understood the attorney dropping his price. It was not a come-on.

His comment exposed me somehow. I suddenly saw that sometimes I manipulated men. The information was uncomfortable. I guessed it was good to know, but I didn't know what to do about it. Bill D. said too that as a self-respecting adult, I didn't need assistance. I need not come across as a little girl.

As someone who desired to be a godly woman, I was to guard myself against using that power to manipulate. But as far as the little girl thing, I guess that was partly due to my voice…Perhaps I could work on confidence.

An important, memorable conversation about my name followed. Bill D. started by holding up a yellow pencil, stating,

"This is a blue pencil."

He went through his little skit about the yellow pencil being a blue pencil several times. Insistent, he asked my name again. I repeated,

"I am Dana Babb. The McKee thing didn't work."

The counselor's voice didn't change. His eyes didn't become laser beams. He began explaining something basic about the folks being treated at Sparks, the nearby mental hospital. They were there largely because they didn't value the truth. On purpose, they deceived someone.

It was like a reverberation was added to his voice. Each of those mentally ill people were there because, at some point, they made up or allowed a lie to avoid facing reality. They called the yellow pencil blue. If one does this lying often enough, one loses the ability to distinguish between what's real and what's imagined.

What Bill D. couldn't have known was that my father could, and did, completely convince himself of untrue things. Things he'd just made up. For instance, Dad believed that my mom was going out on him. For a little while, he frightened us kids that Mom had venereal diseases. He said we kids must carefully clean off the toilet seat before using it after Mom had been home, or we'd get very sick.

After a few months of this, Ray, Douglas, and I figured out that all these appalling claims couldn't be true. Dad believed Mom was dating other men, but how could that be when she came home dead tired from work where she helped the old people at the nursing home? How could she be going out on Dad with some guy at other times? We'd been with her. She went to church, not to meet up with some man.

Dad spent some time in a mental hospital when I was ten. After many irrational, scary episodes, Mom called the State Hospital in Harrisburg, Pennsylvania. They came to get Daddy. The men in white coats arrived, forcing my confused and resistant dad into their station wagon while my five-year-old brother kicked one of the workers in the shins.

I always wondered if Dad's craziness could have been triggered—or at least exaggerated—by lying, maybe when he was young. One lie, I knew about. My young-looking dad told my eighteen-year-old mom a whopper of a lie about his age when they first met. And she didn't find out that Dad was old enough to be her father until she'd married him and was pregnant with Ray.

Before I left that first weekly session, the counselor challenged me on one other thing. He suggested that I put off the divorce. He said a big decision like divorce shouldn't be made under such stressful circumstances as those in which I found myself.

When going to that first appointment, I'd asked the Lord to direct me. I basically promised God that I'd do whatever this guy suggested. Bill D.'s reputation was that he was a genuine Christian. If it panned out that he really was, I'd listen to him and follow his advice. I didn't want to ask opinions from a dozen people. I was too tired.

"Please, just lead me; give me good counsel, God," I prayed.

Leaving that office, I knew I had to do two semi-difficult things:

First, I had to go see the bookkeeper at work. Again. I was back to being D. McKee on my checks. Just until the divorce. It wasn't easy for me to climb those two steps and go into her little office. But those thirty or forty signatures a day would be my undoing if I lied. I had to face reality. Legal reality. Alice looked at me oddly, but she responded,

"Whatever you want, Dana. I'll know it's you."

Second, I had to call the attorney and tell him to hold off on the paperwork we'd talked about. I now planned to wait until after the baby was born. Thinking back, I can understand how the Lord used those tiny steps of obedience to begin turning me back onto the right road. I'd been swerving onto the dangerous, bumpy shoulder, and I needed steering. God was faithfully guiding me, bringing me to himself. He gently led me toward sanity and wholeness when my life was spinning apart.

"Marriage should, I think, always be a little bit hard and new and strange. It should be breaking your shell and going into another world, and a bigger one." – Anne Morrow Lindbergh, American aviator and author

Chapter 12: Our Baby is Born

The baby was coming soon. This birth would be unfamiliar in at least two ways. Not only would a different husband be present, but my family doctor who'd delivered Benji and Ella had stopped delivering babies. So, I also had a new doctor.

It weighed on my mind that Roger wanted to be with me at the birth. I did not like Roger anymore, but he was so excited about this baby…

The pure anticipation he radiated when Roger spoke of our baby appealed to me. But I didn't feel comfortable around Roger; I didn't know what he would be like. Actually, I did know. He would jiggle his knee when sitting. When standing, he'd jump up and down, praising God! He was so enthusiastic.

Baby McKee was "due" January 22, but both my other kids had been born a little later than their estimated dates. The twenty-second drew near. That happened to be the eighth anniversary of Roe v. Wade.

[Speaking of Roe v. Wade, if you've had an abortion, "legal" or not, and you find yourself troubled about it, you are not alone. Many post-abortive women suffer trauma. See abortionmemorial.com.

One important step you can take is to ask God to forgive your sin, and he will forgive you. He can wash the stain of abortion off your conscience and make your heart light and peaceful. Even though this may be a long process, God's peace is available. He waits for you to trust in his great heart of love.

God loves babies. He loves moms too. And dads. And grandmas and granddads. He will help you. Read First John chapter 1. Verse 9 is especially important for you to understand:

"If we confess our sins, he is faithful and just (*just* means "fair") to forgive us our sins and to cleanse us from all unrighteousness."] (Note [xiii])

On January 21, I packed my bag. I'd had a weird episode of feeling faint, and when Mom took my blood pressure, she found it was quite low. So, I went into town and stayed at my cousin Dena's for the evening. She and I took some walks, timed my contractions, and they seemed regular and strengthening. I went to the hospital where the labor slowed, and I fell asleep.

When I was awakened, it was morning. The hospital staff had let me sleep, admitted me, and were breaking my water and putting electrodes on the baby's head when they woke me! What? They didn't even ask if I wanted this. They shushed me and murmured that they were starting my labor.

Drat! I'd had one induced labor and another that started naturally, the natural birth being by far the easier. Well, this baby would be born on the "due date." And this would be a happy day. Lucas was about to make a sad anniversary memorable for something good.

Lucas' birth was the first I'd experienced with monitors. Graphs pumped out of the machine beside me. IV fluids dripped into my arm. Very high tech. Not familiar. (Probably not necessary!)

Should I call Roger? I guessed I should. He was hard to get in touch with on his route, but I decided to try. The number for him was a receptionist in the Sacramento, California, laundry plant on the other side of the mountains. The receptionist would page him from there.

Incredibly, Roger appeared at the hospital less than thirty minutes after I made that phone call. If I'd known, I'd have waited. Nothing seemed to be happening, except for Roger bouncing around. Of course, when a couple of hours passed with "nothing happening," and the Pitocin drip is started, the doctor can make things happen. He ordered the Pitocin turned up.

Suddenly the labor was the familiar hard work that brings the baby. I went from kind of grumpy and bored to very grumpy and very busy. Roger didn't notice the subtle change. I beeped the nurse to tell her that my labor was getting more difficult. The nurse came, checked the graph beside me that showed a gentle bump of a contraction, and tartly contradicted me,

"No. You aren't getting close yet."

I strongly disagreed with her and stated that the machine was wrong. Roger frowned and directed me to be nice to the nurse. I threw him out. Next, I moved the monitor on my laboring belly. The gentle bump on the graph became an off-the-chart, raging rectangle.

Lucas was born not long after. He weighed nearly eight pounds and had dark hair. He had hair! What a beautiful boy! And his dark eyes observed everything right away. Lucas was here, safe and sound. Thank the Lord!

Roger was ecstatic, rejoicing with great joy. Mom was happy to welcome this new little grandson and relieved that there were no complications. By that evening all was well. The next evening the hospital fed us their traditional "Champagne Dinner," which they always served to their new moms and dads. I'd invited Roger, and we had a surprisingly nice dinner with pleasant conversation. No fighting.

I saw Roger more often after the baby was born, but I still couldn't picture us ever getting back together. He came to pick Lucas up some Sundays and kept him for the afternoon, taking him to his old folks' ministry at a nursing home. I'm sure the elderly people loved having the baby to hold. I worried that Roger, being so inexperienced with babies, might wrap him up in a sheet of plastic or some other dangerous thing that would accidentally harm our tiny boy. I was afraid, but I was also impressed at how much Roger loved Lucas. He wouldn't ever leave him.

Pastor Garth, other leadership at church, our friends, and some guys at Roger's work had all begun to advise Roger to divorce me. Even those who didn't believe in divorce felt that, in this case, he needed to move on. We'd been separated for five of the first ten months of our marriage.

One day in February, Roger said to me, "Maybe we do need to divorce."

He'd uttered those words before. Lots of times. But not in over five months. Not since that day when dropping me off for my "last day of work." And not in this sad, serious, exhausted tone.

It got my attention. For the first time, I wondered if I really wanted him to stop pursuing me.

The thing about my feelings for Roger was that he now felt like a brother. I loved him like I loved Ray or Douglas or Cliff. How could that work? He left. I prayed.

The next time I saw Roger coming, my heart skipped a beat. No joke! It was a miracle. The spark was back in my heart again. The thought hit me,

"Whoa! He is so handsome!"

It startled me that the revulsion I'd felt for my husband was completely gone. It wasn't there anymore. What transformation! I didn't tell him right away. It was exciting, but what if it was just a fluke?

Later, Roger confessed to me that before I left him, he'd been praying I would leave. (Great...Mr. Church Elder couldn't leave, though he was done with our relationship too.)

My husband told me that his heart toward me changed when he fasted and prayed for me. Before God, he realized he had been praying the wrong prayer.

"God, please make her leave," became "God, please bring Dana back."

Roger had gone to God in earnest with his appeal for restoration:

"We got married before you, Lord. You bring my wife back to me. I will trust you."

The big change that miraculously came about in Roger after the kids and I left him was now being duplicated in me. This was in answer to Roger's prayers. My new interest in Roger wasn't some hormonal glitch. It was a miracle. Resurrection wasn't something I could make up my mind to accomplish, but God could and did raise the dead! My feelings for my husband that had died were renewed.

Bill D. cautioned us about jumping too quickly into our renewed relationship, but it seemed to us that we needed to be together to work on the marriage. We were optimistic.

For our first anniversary celebration, we planned to meet for dinner at a restaurant in Reno, between his apartment to the west, and Fernley to the east, where the kids and I lived.

Matthew 6:34 "Therefore do not be anxious about tomorrow, for tomorrow will be anxious for itself. Sufficient for the day is its own trouble."

Part 2 – Me, a Real McKee

Chapter 13: Reconciliation With Complications

Crazy, the things that can happen on an ordinary, sunny Friday. Late that day, the one when Roger and I were meeting to celebrate our first anniversary, Mr. Babb went to jail. He'd found his wife in the arms of another man, and Mr. Babb ended up in prison on attempted murder charges. He'd used a knife.

My husband moved back in with us. Amazingly, we were happy together. We now had the unusual complication of my needing to take the kids to see Mr. Babb about once a month for sixteen or eighteen months. It wasn't the smoothest way to move our reconciled marriage forward, but Roger let me go. And he never hassled me about going so far out of my way to care of my former husband, who definitely suffered from PTSD. He needed to see Benji and Ella to keep hope in his life. So, I regularly drove the kids to visit their dad in prison. And Roger trusted me. More importantly, he relied on God.

As Roger and I were reunited, he invited me to go with him on a vacation called an Excursion Trip. He'd mentioned it several times before we even got back together. An Excursion Ticket involved one plane ticket, but somehow included lots of stops over a couple of weeks. As our love was restored and renewed, it began to sound exciting.

Roger planned to see his family and friends in the South and told me I could choose some stops too. I chose to see my brother, Ray, who was living with his family in southern Pennsylvania. We were already scheduled to be in Washington, D. C., for two or three days. Roger decided D. C. was close enough to Pennsylvania to work out a visit with Ray without booking another flight.

We planned to take Lucas to meet Roger's mom and to visit some of Roger's aunts and an uncle. And he wanted us to go see some of his old friends in Miami, Florida, as well.

I'd never flown before. The take-off from Reno frightened and thrilled me, but the quick, smooth ride was amazing. We landed in Las Vegas to pick up some passengers, and then we headed for our first stop, Atlanta, Georgia.

Again, the take-off made me grab Roger's hand, shut my eyes tight, and commit my life (and death) to the Lord of heaven. The four-hour flight was uneventful, almost like not moving at all, until we approached Hartsfield International Airport. Interrupting our descent, we suddenly pulled up. Our plane began circling the airport, flying low, spotlights sweeping the underside of the plane. After an hour in that holding pattern, the pilot calmly spoke over the intercom,

"Pensacola says our landing gear appears to be locked, and it is safe to try our landing. Flight attendants will instruct you as to crash positions."

Crash positions?! How could I secure and protect a three-month-old in this emergency? I cuddled Lucas as closely to me as I could with one arm and braced with the other while wondering, "What does Pensacola, Florida, have to do with our landing in Atlanta, Georgia?!"

I prayed silently for mercy, help, and safety. As we broke through the low, ragged clouds, we saw emergency vehicles all along the foam-covered runway. No one on that flight yelled or screamed. Prayers rose from the quiet plane, and we landed smoothly. Thank you, God!

Roger hadn't seen his mom and stepdad in five years, and their north Georgia home was our first stop. Dorothy loved seeing Roger and meeting me too. She fed us biscuits with butter and field peas flavored with salt pork. We drank her sweetest-of-sweet iced tea and all kinds of goodies, some of which were unfamiliar to me.

Dorothy was well, but she so cherished little Lucas that she wore a mask when she held him the first day we were there. She wanted to make sure she would not give the baby any germs. Dorothy was pretty excited about her new little grandson.

Aunt Pat, later called "Granny Pat" by our kids, loaded her refrigerator with delicious food and let us have her cute apartment while we visited Greenville, South Carolina. Pat stayed with her cousin nearby, stopping in often over the two days we were there. She was the perfect embodiment of southern hospitality in her short, wide little self. Playing with the baby, she had him laughing out loud! At three months! Aunt Pat was the first person, besides Roger, who made me begin to know that it was good to be a McKee.

Roger's dad had passed away before I got a chance to meet him. But we visited Uncle George, who was Roger's father's brother. George and Aunt Niki put us up in the extra bedroom of their lovely home, Quarters One at the Soldiers' and Airmen's Home in Washington D.C. What a classy couple! Aunt Niki made a delicious Chicken Tetrazzini dish for supper the evening we stayed with them, and she wrote out her recipe for me.

I did get to introduce Roger and baby Lucas to my brother, Ray, his wife, and their two little children, M.J. and Richard. Ray drove down from York, Pennsylvania, to meet up with us.

The day we visited with them ended up being memorable for a series of minor mishaps, and Roger afterwards referred to it as "Dana Day." Toward the end of Dana Day, Ray's car broke down. So, we were stuck beside the road. After considering possible solutions for quite a while, and still no end in sight, Roger called a cab and our family drove off, leaving Ray and his family stranded.

It escapes me now, why we felt we had to go and leave them. I was probably getting worn out, and Roger was simply caring for me and our little Lucas. I know my brother didn't need me to hold his hand to get through that troublesome day, nor did he need us to fix his car. But that was a disappointing ending to that visit. (A postscript—Ray found his calling, ended up in a great job, has four terrific kids now, and he's driven beautiful, dependable cars for years.)

Our last excursion stop brought us to the palm trees and blue water of Miami, Florida. We had a lot of fun with Roger's friends there. And meeting Roger's old girlfriend was not as stressful as I thought it might be. Her parents, aunt, and brother showered us with kindness, and L. and her brother took us snorkeling in the Keys. Amazing sights lie under that clear, warm water.

Two tiny bits of offense lodged in my consciousness from the Excursion Trip, though. When Roger first invited me to come along on his adventurous trip to the South, he told me to come up with additional destinations. Maybe I waited too long to convey my wishes, but he didn't adjust our flights. (Note [xiv])

That reminded me of Proverbs 25:14, "Like clouds and wind without rain is a man who boasts of a gift he does not give."

Roger does give great gifts. The whole vacation was a generous present. And he did map out a part of the trip for visiting my brother. But when that one day became long and uninteresting to Roger, and hard for all of us, he named the day after me…Then Roger had me meet the woman he'd lived with for a year and arranged for us to stay with her family for a couple of days.

The old girlfriend was smaller, thinner and more muscular. She seemed to find it easier to smile, had whiter teeth, and was more talented than I in artistic ways. I liked her. I liked her family. It was good that Roger wanted me to meet all these dear people from his past. And he obviously didn't think I compared unfavorably with L. But I tripped and fell into the traps of jealousy and comparison. And I wasn't sure how to stop those jealous comparisons in my mind.

"A great marriage is not when the 'perfect couple' comes together. It is when an imperfect couple learns to enjoy their differences." – Dave Meurer, American humorist. (Quote found at goodreads.com/quotes/22136, accessed 04-25-2022)

Chapter 14: Life in Stead. And Reno. And Devil's Pond.

We moved to Stead, Nevada, fifteen miles north of Reno. Roger got his great camera out while we lived there and took portraits of our kids that captured their personalities. He'd worked as a full-time photographer several years before this, yet now as a route salesman, Roger almost never had time to express his creative side and take photos of anything. In the new duplex he found the time. I loved his use of natural light and the poses he came up with. Roger knew what F stop and other settings would be right to get the exposure he wanted.

Adjusting to my husband involved making the bed. I was a fair housekeeper, at least for the parts of the house that "show." But closets, drawers, and bedrooms were far down the list. After all, the beds were going to get messed up again each night. I'd straighten something else and just close the bedroom doors. Roger was not a perfectly organized soul either, but one day he came home, found the bed unmade—again, and asked why I didn't make the bed.

"Did you notice the stuff I did get done?"

Roger calmly reiterated, "I don't care if nothing else gets done; I would like our bed made."

From then on, I made the bed. I may allow our bedroom to become the catchall, book storage, junk room for a while, but I make the bed.

While I was successfully beginning to adapt to my man, the kids were faced with adjusting to yet another school. That change was especially important for Benji. I knew from my own experience how hard school moves could be. Always being the new kid wasn't easy. We knew we weren't going be living in Stead long, so we ferried the kids back and forth a bit.

When we went to enroll the kids at the public school near our proposed location, I worried about so much change for Ella, who was going into first grade. But at the parents' night/open house, where we met the new teachers, I realized it was Benji who was even more vulnerable. He was scared, and the teacher they assigned him was terrible. She didn't seem to be enjoying herself at all. Maybe she should've resigned years earlier. That woman wasn't able to be welcoming to my son even when I was standing right there with him. What made it worse, he'd just survived a similar teacher at Fernley Elementary.

We checked out the room of the teacher in another fourth-grade class down the hall. She was great! I went to the principal the next day and insisted that they change my son's assigned class. Office staff told me that if they moved Benji, another student would have to be placed with that irritable woman. But I stood firm. Ben reports that when I took his side and made a fuss about that teacher, it gave him the determination to stand up for himself in a new way. He'd lay aside his nickname. When asked his name in the new classroom, he replied,

"My name is Ben."

Both Ella and Ben had good teachers there. They did well, getting great grades. Thank you, God, again and again for taking care of us.

We moved into a Reno community, next door to friends, Nancy and Jerry. I'd known them briefly at Life Center. They'd found Sparks Foursquare while I'd been away those long months of our separation. In fact, they had been helping pray for Roger's difficult, bad wife, not knowing it was me. (I'm thankful for all prayers.) We got to be close. Our kids played together and went to school together. We all attended church together.

While it was a daily blessing to live next to friends, a rare treat came in the form of a week-long visit from Aunt Pat in the spring. We had lots of fun with her.

Baby Lucas was probably first in her heart, but she loved all the kids and showed a genuine interest in each one.

Pat took Roger and me to Harrah's to see Wayne Newton's show. We took her to breakfast out at Pyramid Lake, which was a meaningful place to Roger. He was pleased to show her that salt lake where he loved to fish.

It meant so much to us that Pat boarded a plane, flew clear across the United States, and came to see us.

That summer we drove across the US, from Nevada to Georgia to visit Roger's mom, introducing Ben and Ella in person. I began to see that the South was charming and beautiful. I'd lived in the West, the East, and the Mid-west, but never the South. I discovered that people don't need to sound alike. Are we less smart or more educated because of an accent? No.

The next spring, we had to move to Georgia. Roger's mom had suddenly gotten very sick and wasn't expected to live long. In preparation for the big move to be near Grandma Dorothy, we quickly staged a yard sale.

The sale day was partly bright, partly snow flurries. I didn't grab a jacket, just ran back and forth from the house to the front yard all day, working at selling our belongings. We made a good bit of money, but I got thoroughly chilled. That evening I remember shivering, not able to get warm. Soon, I was totally weak, fatigued, coughing. Ben got sick too. With his asthma, he often had those symptoms. But with both of us sick, we huddled together in Roger's and my big waterbed. This is my favorite memory of that time.

I told Ben a joke, whispering and coughing:

"There was a guy buying cheese in a grocery store. No, wait—there were two guys, both buying cheese. Somehow, the one guy accidentally got the other guy's cheese and left the store. When chased by the other, he ran, trying to lose the crazy guy chasing. He got away. Breathless, he made it home. His wife asked, 'What kind of cheese did you get?' He answered, 'I thought it was cheddar, but a guy screamed at me for blocks, yelling 'That's not yo' cheese! That's not yo' cheese.' I guess it's nacho cheese."

We both laughed so hard, we were gasping, "Stop making me laugh; I can't breathe!"

Maybe you had to be there.

The doctor gave me an antibiotic after finding that I had pneumonia, and I started getting better. Even so, I could barely move. I had no energy. Our church friends packed us while I lay on the couch, watching them scurry past. They wrapped and carefully boxed all our belongings. When we finally unpacked, I found that some of the dishes in newsprint were not mine but were from meals our kind friends had brought over to support our family while I was sick. I loved those thoughtful folks.

When we set off on our move, Roger, Ben, and Ella drove across country in a large moving truck with all our belongings, even the VW Rabbit, packed inside. Roger told me the kids started the "Are-we-there-yet?" question before he got to Carson City.

Since I was still weak, Lucas and I stayed with my mom for a few days and then caught a flight to Atlanta. Our yard sale money was just enough to pay the doctor, get medicine, and buy two airline tickets. Five days later for Roger and the older kids, five hours later for me and Lucas, we all arrived at Hartsfield Airport. No crash positions required this time, thank the Lord.

We first visited Grandma Dorothy for a couple days and then headed for Devil's Pond, Georgia, where Aunt Pat allowed us to stay temporarily in her summer place.

"Almost no one is foolish enough to imagine that he automatically deserves great success in any field of activity; yet almost everyone believes that he automatically deserves success in marriage." – Sydney J. Harris, American journalist

Quote taken from *Worth Repeating* © Copyright 2003 by Bob Kelly. Published by Kregel Publications, Grand Rapids, MI. Used by permission of the publisher. All rights reserved.

Chapter 15: Manners. Work. Georgia Girl.

We put our stuff in storage and collapsed in Pat's sweet, comfortably furnished trailer. Situated in a cool, breezy, Georgia, pine grove, this was the perfect place to pause and to complete the school year. Ella was finishing second grade and Ben fifth.

We began encountering a cultural difference. A terse note came home from school one day. In it a teacher chided us that the kids needed to be taught to be polite.

Hey! Some of their first words were "please" and "thank you"—are you kidding me? But since I hadn't taught them to say "Ma'am" and "Sir," they "had no manners."

In Oglethorpe County we were near two of Roger's aunts, Dorothy's older sisters. Aunt Annette often found fun toys at yard sales, giving them to our kids. And Ben loved to fish in Aunt Lillie's nearby pond.

Looking for a place where we could move in, unpack, and settle down proved to take diligence and patience. We answered ads for homes for rent around Augusta. Every time we could, we drove down there. It was a pleasure to go, as Augusta, Georgia, is the most gorgeous place ever in spring. Graceful dogwood trees bloom white, with dazzling, pink azaleas flowering beneath them. Everything is green…so startlingly different from arid Nevada.

But house-hunting was frustrating. What we could afford was so bad. How could people offer to rent something so sorry for that much? We continued to enjoy the comfort of Pat's trailer.

Thankfully, Grandma Dorothy had rallied and gotten some better. Whenever we could, we made the two-hour drive to see her, and she loved it. She loved us. She doted on our kids, all of them. The medications she had to take made her uncomfortable with some serious side effects, but she was doing pretty well. She couldn't work outside her home, and that bothered her. But she kept up her house, laundry, and meals.

Dorothy didn't understand why I stayed home. To her way of thinking, taking care of our kids and all responsibilities at home could be fitted around a job. She told me I should "help Roger."

"There are jobs out there; work at Roy Roger's until you find something better," she said. (Roy Roger's was a fast-food place.)

Dorothy had worked in the fields hoeing and chopping cotton when she was a little girl and had worked at sewing factories ever since. She put Roger in day care at three months old so she could get back to her sewing job. She'd never heard of a modern woman being content to work inside her home, taking care of her husband and kids. My mother-in-law may have been a bit concerned that I was lazy.

Roger didn't stay in Aunt Pat's trailer the whole time the kids and I were there. He went to work. He'd figured out a job transfer to continue with Aratex, a Georgia laundry company related to Red Star in Nevada. So, after a brief time off, Roger drove to Savannah.

There he found that they didn't know about him. They'd forgotten Roger's boss's call recommending him as a great route salesman.

"Who are you again? Just wait here."

"What do you do? Work in the plant?" (Plant work is unskilled and low paying, not something worth commuting 130 miles one-way for.)

"No. Remember? I'm Roger McKee, the route sales guy who is going to build up your business in Augusta."

The General Manager, beginning to remember that he'd talked to a General Manager who called from California two weeks earlier said,

"Okay. Wait here a minute…"

This was a bit scary for Roger, to say the least. And even after they did arrange for him to use a small van and a job, it was still "life on the edge" for us. Roger didn't tell me until much later how precarious it all was. They invented a spot for him. Roger was called "The Man with the Van" by the boss in Savannah. If he could sell laundry service, great. If not, he wouldn't get paid. It was all up to Roger who had to knock on doors. There were no salespeople making support calls, just Roger.

55

God gave him favor, and Roger started building up his route. And he got paid.

Aunt Pat came and got me at the trailer one pretty day in June saying, "I'll take you to Augusta. We'll find you a house."

She was right; there it was, beside Lake Olmstead. It was perfect. We moved into a quiet, older, well-maintained neighborhood.

The single car garage became the Aratex Augusta, Georgia depot (not that they paid us extra). Bags of smelly, dirty uniforms, mops, and mats stayed in our car port all week until Roger could make his trip to Savannah, drop those off, and get the clean items. (I'd never seen roaches anywhere I had lived, but with the industrial laundry dirties right outside the house, I was soon introduced.)

Our neighbors from Reno, Nancy and Jerry, moved in with us in June. We had four adults and six kids in a home with four bedrooms and two baths. For their dog, Jerry built a ramshackle dog run out back. It was good to have our friends there, but it was wild.

The dining room was a small, separate room. Our round dining table fit, but it was only big enough for the kids. So, we fed them at the table while we adults ate in the living room in front of the TV. Our children really did lose all their manners during those five months of togetherness. (Table manners, anyway.)

I began to pray for a table that would seat us all. I prayed for a specific pine trestle table like one that I'd seen in a house-cleaning client's home. (Nancy and I had run a small business where we cleaned houses together in Reno.) The table I wanted was constructed of solid pine and stained a dark mahogany. An Ethan Allen table. It had matching side chairs, two captain's chairs, and a bench. When I'd admired it, the lady who owned that table had warned me,

"Don't ever get pine like this one. It's too soft. Get maple."

But I hoped and prayed for a table just like hers. I didn't care that it would show the scars of kids growing up around it. And...can you guess? The Lord found it for me, not that year, but the next. There it was in the nickel ads. Hooray!

"For sale: an Ethan Allen-type, solid pine trestle table, stained a very dark mahogany. Also, two captain's chairs, two side chairs, and a bench."

It was a deacon's bench, not backless. But the set was perfect for us. And it was in like-new condition. The table also had two leaves, so we could extend it to fit a crowd! (And she let me make payments! Miraculous.)

Nancy and I both got pregnant that fall. We continued our cleaning business, this time tidying up the school affiliated with the Foursquare Gospel Church on Tubman Home Road. I did the bathrooms. Not pleasant, but my friend, Nancy, had morning sickness, and I didn't. That's where I learned to use a plastic bag to get huge balls of bathroom tissue and other stuff out of toilets. Nancy cleaned the classrooms and everything else. She was the speedy cleaning woman, a sanitizing tornado that whirled through and brought sparkle and order. I was the slow, polish-everything plodder.

We put the kids into the private Christian school, and that's where our smart, sweet Ella skipped third grade. Her teacher offered thoughtful little incentives for the third-grade learners, but Ella constantly got them all. She won all the pennies, all the stickers, everything. The teacher approached us, asking if we would consider putting her up a grade. Roger and I agreed. The fourth-grade teacher agreed. I warned our little daughter that she might not get all A's at first until she caught up, but I encouraged her to go for it. She rose to the challenge, and unbelievably, she never dropped her grades at all. In fact, Ella got an award at the end of the year for finishing with the highest GPA in grades 4-12! We were very proud of our girl.

Nancy gave birth to their baby boy, Andrew, in May. I had our little Georgia girl, Jayna, in June. Both were beautiful and healthy.

Roger's deal with Aratex was that when the business around Augusta was built up with enough sales and delivery routes to be a district, he'd be promoted and become District Manager. He worked incredibly hard to make that happen. Roger was a faithful, conscientious employee. After a year of growing the business to district-size, Augusta needed a District Manager. The boss in Savannah hired an outside guy as DM over Augusta. Roger quit.

"Marriage should be a duet – when one sings, the other claps." – Joe Murray, American animator, producer, voice actor (Found at brainyquotes.com, accessed 04/25/22)

Chapter 16: More Moves

Another laundry company hired my husband, and he worked with them for the next year. Even with legal, covenant restrictions disallowing Roger to sell service to his known customers, he did well at Uniform Rental. Roger continued working for several months in Augusta. But when a sales job with Uniform Rental opened up in the Atlanta area, we moved three hours away.

Jayna was four months old for that move. After we got situated, my sister came to stay with us for a couple of months. On a sunny Saturday morning when our baby Jayna was eight and a half months old, Roger and Carol claimed she walked, ran even. Excited, they brought the baby to the ball field where I was practicing softball with our church's women's team.

"Dana, come watch this! Jayna was walking between us!"

They put the baby down and encouraged her to "walk to Daddy!" She sat down.

"Come on, Jayna. Walk to Aunt Carol."

Our happy baby sat down again and pat-a-caked. I got into the action and tried to get Jayna to walk to me. Nope. At first, I thought maybe she was shy; too many strangers in the audience for her to perform her astonishing feat. On second thought, I doubt it was that. By the time she was two, Jayna feared nothing. No height, no river current, nothing at all!

The house in Powder Springs had a white, picket fence around the front lawn. We got a puppy whose wiry, white coat had a couple of well-placed black spots that made him look rather like the dog in the old RCA Victor ad. So, we named him Victor. (Jerry and Nancy's Springer Spaniel whelped twelve precious, half-breed puppies! Victor was one of those.)

Lucas loved Victor and rescued him when he got himself stuck getting through the fence. When the pup was little, he'd easily run right between those pickets. But growing fast, he became too large to fit. Our puppy couldn't figure out what had happened to that fence. Why couldn't he get through? What a puzzle for a yelping little dog! Later, Victor became Ben's dog, his faithful buddy.

Ben and Ella were back to public schools. We enrolled Ben in Tapp for seventh grade, and Ella in Compton for fifth. The instruction in those schools leaned left, toward liberal indoctrination, and the kids on Ella's bus were not nice. They were abusive. And the school did nothing about the kids who threatened her. Meeting Ella as she got off the bus trying not to cry, I heard some of the awful insults they were yelling at my girl. It was frustrating to feel so helpless when Ella was humiliated and scared.

The bad school situations were not the only issue there. We found that a nearly commission-only pay structure was stressful for Roger. He did well with sales, but no matter how well he did today, tomorrow he started over. He stressed out about how to provide for us. Roger began having painful ulcer symptoms. Aratex (renamed Aramark around that time) had some District Manager openings that offered a possible promotion and a salary. Getting away from the commission-only pay structure would be a big relief. Roger took a DM job and went back to work for the big laundry company.

The small Assembly of God church where we fellowshipped was one of the few things in that place we would miss. We became life-long friends with Rob, the pastor.

As Gainesville, Georgia's new District Manager, Roger moved us away from the Atlanta area. We bought some land in north Georgia where we planned to build a house. Until we could complete that project, we'd live somewhere cheap. Looking through newspaper ads, I found it. This place sounded cheap-but-adequate, and it included a new washer and dryer. I talked to the owner on the phone, and she gave me directions. She said that a student had been living in the house. So, a couple of people might be there but would be leaving.

I drove to Commerce, Georgia, and checked it out. Her directions seemed easy to follow, and the place was great. It was amazingly neat and tidy for what the owner was asking. I sent the deposit and first month's rent. I had our mail redirected and the power company notified. The electricity would be turned on before we arrived.

Roger's route guys came from the Gainesville depot and loaded up our household things in laundry trucks. Four trucks and two cars held all our belongings, four kids, our birds, and Victor the dog. We drove fifty miles up Highway 85 and exited onto Maysville Road. It was dark by the time everybody caravanned to the rural area where we were headed, taking the windy, country road. The whole train followed me to the new house. When we arrived, there were lights on. People were in there! Roger knocked on the door, and explained that we were moving in.

"We were told you would be out by now."

Confused, they answered, "No, this is our house. Oh, you mean the place up the road."

They gave us precise directions.

Realization hit! We were moving to a place we'd never seen.

When I drove to the place a month earlier, I thought I'd accounted for every element of the directions: the nearby tree farm, the white siding, etc. However, I forgot about the stone chimney.

The place I'd rented for us was a dilapidated little shack nearly hidden in tangled, waist-high grass. The power was not turned on. We looked around with flashlights. Watch out! An open well two feet across yawned in the dense, front-yard weeds. The worn, dirty house leaned in on itself. Floor coverings were linoleum that had almost no surface left on them. Cleaning would be worse than trying to polish a dirt floor. I could never put our little one-year-old daughter down in that house.

Roger's route guys took the loaded trucks back to the depot and parked them for the night while we considered what to do. We called Aunt Pat. Was her little trailer still unoccupied? Could we stay there again for a few weeks? Pat agreed, and we found ourselves back in Oglethorpe County.

The Commerce landlady gave us back all our deposit and rent money. Nancy and Jerry generously kept the dog and the birds for us until we could get situated. While there, Victor ate the birds. We'd clipped their wings so they couldn't fly away like their parents did soon after the babies hatched. Someone accidentally left the cage open. This loss was especially sad to Ben and me. He and I had lost a lot of sleep rearing those two naked little monsters into colorful, tame, peach-faced lovebirds. Nancy, Jerry, and the boys were sorry too.

"Love is friendship that has caught on fire. It is quiet understanding, mutual confidence, sharing and forgiving. It is loyalty through good and bad times. It settles for less than perfection and makes allowances for human weaknesses." – Ann Landers, American writer and columnist (Quate found at Parade.com. Also at brainyquote.com, accessed 04-25-2022)

Chapter 17: Home as a Prefix

The refunded deposit gave me an unclaimed chunk of money. This meant I could homeschool the kids; I could buy their books! I was intrigued by homeschooling and had read up on the new phenomenon before we left Reno. Though almost nobody did it back then, I thought this would be good for our family. And perfect timing. We were going to have to move again, a couple more times.

Homeschooling would give the kids some continuity. There would be no possibility of mean, threatening kids on the bus, and I would have the freedom to teach my kids history, geography, language, spelling, math, science, and Bible from a Christian perspective. I also hoped to teach them practical, real-life skills.

There were only two curriculum sellers I knew of at the time. From one of them I ordered three whole classrooms worth of instruction for Ben's eighth grade, Ella's sixth grade, and four-year-old Lucas's Kindergarten. It was exciting. And overwhelming. The boxes and boxes of binders and books taught me how to teach. Starting in Granny Pat's tiny trailer, I began studying.

Before long, we all dove into the books. Everybody studied hard while Jayna, who was one year old, climbed on us. I'd promised the kids swim lessons and field trips, but those never came together. I got caught up in the new thing we were doing and forgot that I wanted to "home" school. I tried to reproduce classroom learning to the extent that I wanted the children to complete every page of every textbook and workbook. To say it was a super-hard, intense year would almost be an understatement. In retrospect, I hate it that I didn't adapt our homeschool to real life. Nor did I figure out how to include the fun stuff. Now I was the one promising like "clouds and wind without rain." Proverbs 25:14.

We bought seven acres of woods not far from the Chattahoochee River in Lula, Georgia, and started clearing and home-building.

We moved out of Pat's little place and into a tiny two-bedroom, one-bath place in Flowery Branch, nearer Roger's work and the building project.

Our house was supposed to be finished by Thanksgiving, then by Christmas, then by Easter. We moved in on June 2. It was great to finally be in our cozy, new home, with space for a couple more bedrooms and another bath in the walk-out basement. We added those later. Jayna turned two in the new house. Lucas, we kept home instead of putting him into the optional kindergarten. We enrolled the older kids back in public school that fall, Ella in seventh grade, Ben in ninth.

One very cool bonus about Roger having gone back to work for Aramark was the regular sales contests. Prize trips were offered for contest qualifiers. Roger worked very hard, God blessed him, and he always qualified. Sometimes he won the entire contest!

The prize trip in spring 1986 was a four-day cruise to the Bahamas. It was the best cruise ever. We faced a hurdle, though, when we got to the boat that almost ruined things. Roger was supposed to bring along contraception stuff. He didn't. And believe it or not, none could be bought on board our Carnival Cruise ship. When I unpacked in our teeny quarters and found there were no precautionary measures in our luggage, I folded my arms and was about to say,

"Oh, well, Buddy. Whatever."

(Isn't it a little strange the way we fear babies?! In our culture, we do. Nearly all of us, at one time or another, have been stressed at the thought of bringing another child into the world.)

That refusal of intimacy wouldn't have been right, and I knew it. Opening my arms back up, I allowed my husband and myself relaxation and intimacy. We enjoyed the freest, most beautiful time together on that cruise. I decided not to worry about preventing a baby. We were in God's hands, and he could give us another child if he saw fit. We didn't get pregnant that month, but we started hoping for one more child.

We soon got pregnant with Baby #5. Grandma Dorothy wasn't happy at first, worrying about how we'd care for so many kids. But we rejoiced and gave thanks to God for the new little one. And Grandma Dorothy came around later. Believe me! She loved all her grandkids. My mom, Grandma Audrey, was always happy about baby news. She was busy working and rearing Carol's daughter, Amy. But she visited us when she could, and she had faith in God, and maybe in us too, that we could care for one more.

I had another new doctor. Jayna's birth had involved a complication with Pitocin, the labor-inducing hormone. My blood sugar fell; my blood pressure dropped precipitously too. It was scary and completely exhausting. But I made it through that labor, and our baby girl was born beautiful and healthy.

All our precious kids were born healthy after comparatively short labors. So, I wanted to try a homebirth and avoid the hospital pitfalls if possible. I did my research; I'd be a good candidate for this. I just had to find an experienced midwife with whom I felt comfortable. The second one we interviewed was the one.

Living twenty minutes from the hospital, I continued to see my new obstetrician. He'd be my back-up plan if something came up that would necessitate a hospital birth.

Our baby waited until the last possible day to be born, my obstetrician insisting that he induce labor the following day. Rather uneventfully, Baby #5 was born in our bedroom. Mom always came to be with me for my births. So, she was downstairs with our other kids watching and re-watching a movie. At three years old, Jayna said it was a scary one. *Dune*?

I loved the homebirth experience. I loved that there was no transition home from a hospital. After the hard work of labor, I felt an unrivaled, satisfying glow and contentment. That birth-day proved to be way less hectic than those on which I welcomed our other children.

Our baby wasn't named for an entire week; Roger and I had trouble agreeing about that small detail...his name.

For this sweet, dark-haired, grey-eyed child, I finally resorted to arm-twisting. I reminded Roger that at one particularly difficult time during the birth, he'd promised,

"You are doing the work; name this baby whatever you want."

He remembered and agreed. What I wanted was a good, Bible name—Barnabas. He is our "Son of Encouragement."

"…it is interesting that the Bible has a whole book celebrating erotic love in marriage. It shows what a high view the Bible has of sexual intimacy in marriage. It speaks of delight and contentment—a love that is wholehearted and passionate—holding nothing back."

That is part of a commentary on *Song of Songs*, chapters 1-4. For more, look online for a devotional called the Bible in One Year 2021 with Nicky Gumbel, Day 230. (Note [xv])

Chapter 18: Forgiveness & Football, Band & Karate

Roger and I got to go to a biblical seminar I'd heard about long before and always wished to attend. The Basic Conference was a big blessing. As the lecturer exhorted and encouraged us to live our Christian faith, I learned about submission to God-given authority. He explained that when one under authority disagrees with the person who has responsibility for them, or is in authority over them, that is where submission begins.

Submission to one's proper authority, whether parents, husband, employer, government, etc., is done as a sign of faith in God. God is the real authority. He is the only One who knows everything and can make no mistakes. His rules for leadership and submission are foundational for long-term relationships. Short-term, peer relationships don't need a head. But for orderly, peaceful structures of society to stand strong and steady through various turmoils, we need leaders. (A real problem is that we have seen few models of good leadership in daily life. And bad examples range from deceitful manipulators to pushy tyrants to pushovers who will not assume responsibility.)

We need followers too. We often disagree. We lead or submit or help imperfectly. That is when we must remember that God is the real boss. When I am in authority, I only rightly lead as a steward of God's authority. I'm just a manager, working for the Lord.

When I am under authority, my trust in God not only kicks in when there is strong disagreement, but I must also, in faithfulness to hold up my end of the relationship, express my viewpoint to said authority. After that, I may confidently submit my will as evidence of my faith in my Master, the Lord who made me. My trust is not in the fallible human who leads, but in the omniscient, omnipresent, eternal God of heaven.

That conference was where I first understood the key that submission really matters in disagreement. And it's such an important element in the Lord's design for long-term relationships. I can submit to Roger because I trust God.

The speaker's emphasis on accepting one's parents and the importance of realizing and appreciating that God put you in the home situation where you were born and/or reared, that was memorable for me. There is no happenstance with a child's conception.

The seminar speaker also taught on forgiveness of parents. Although I'd done that, I needed to forgive my dad some more. I figured that was part of what Jesus meant when he said we should forgive "seventy times seven" (Matthew 18:22). We are to keep on forgiving. It means, if a remembered incident or person still makes my stomach knot up, I can choose to forgive again. And again. That was what Mom had always taught me. But the seminar reminder was good.

We went to the follow-up conference sometime after the basic seminar. Roger and I took Ben and Ella along, teenagers rolling their eyes. Afterward, we hosted several related weekly meetings in our home. During and after one of those home meetings, something remarkable happened.

This particular home meeting was on scriptural instructions to forgive. Ben spoke up. He had trouble forgiving his dad for leaving. We talked about it and about how forgiveness frees us from the offender. And, gently, we pointed out that God requires this choice.

Jesus highlighted forgiveness in the Lord's Prayer in Matthew 6:5-15. He taught the disciples to pray, "...forgive us our debts, as we also have forgiven our debtors." Matthew 6:12

There, our Master teaches us that to be forgiven by God for our sins, we must forgive. Heavy stuff. It's a difficult but crucial measure we can decide to take. And isn't forgiving part of the "obedience of faith" spoken of by Paul the apostle in Romans 16:26?

We prayed for each other, asking God to help Ben get past his inability to forgive.

Ella wanted prayer too. She asked that we pray that she would hear from her dad.

For four years, Mr. Babb had completely dropped off our radar screen. He'd moved, and I knew of no way to contact him if I'd needed to...if one of the kids had had an emergency. But that four years was about to end.

That night he called! Out of the blue, Mr. Babb wanted to begin sending child support! And he had a plan in place for settling with me for child support arrears. If I would agree to his plan, he wanted to come see the kids.

Wild. God heard and had already begun to fulfill Ben and Ella's hearts' desires before they even prayed. God is faithful and fabulous! It is true that he cares for his people.

The Bible says: "You do not have, because you do not ask." (James 4:2).

Ben's other big ask was to play football. He made repeated requests. But I couldn't agree with his participation in that rough sport. I was afraid. I felt I could not stand by and allow our son to get injured. Ben was so fully committed to whatever he tried...I knew he would get hurt. I prayed, but I had no peace about letting him play. Roger thought Ben would be fine playing football, but he listened to my concerns and didn't override me. He extended grace to me.

Then I read a book. It came in the mail as one of my monthly book club choices. It was *Men and Marriage* by George Gilder. Mr. Gilder explained in the pages of that book how important it was for Ben to play football. *Men and Marriage* surely helped my understanding of Roger too, as Mr. Gilder made several fascinating points about the civilizing of men through marriage.

But my main take-away was this: young guys must have a challenging outlet, usually something that pushes them physically. They are designed for adventure, and they need to struggle to hunt or war or grapple with something huge and meaningful and difficult, and something that makes them part of a team. It's "a man thing." If they don't have this outlet, they go a little crazy.

That book was, to me, God's answer to a prayer I'd prayed:

"Lord, let me either have peace about Ben playing football, or let him be okay with not playing. Because I am going to forbid him to play. It won't make me the most popular mom, not that that matters...Help us, please."

I thank God for his timely, clear answer.

Ben participated in Academic Team and wrestling, and he did play on his high school football team. He was a committed, focused linebacker. Ben got hurt. He had arthroscopic surgery to repair a problem in his knee. And other injuries also sent him to physical therapy. One time I was scared that his neck was hurt, but he was fine. Thank God!

Ella skillfully played clarinet in the high school band, and she participated in drill team. Both she and Ben worked part time at nearby restaurants. And Ella was my built-in babysitter. She did all that, as well as countless chores, and maintained outstanding grades in her academics. We were proud of our girl though she and I waded into difficult mom/oldest daughter crazy times. We struggled to communicate. At least, we yelled a great deal.

For first grade, Lucas went to public school, where he learned to read. He did very well there. But he seemed in danger of becoming a lost boy - lost in the middle of our gang. The big kids had to be taken to school and work. The little ones could cry and quickly get what they needed. Our middle boy played T-ball and liked that, but he dreamed of learning martial arts after watching the *Karate Kid* movie. The Lord provided a way, and we signed him up for karate. Lucas loved it. Later he had the opportunity to switch from karate to Tae-kwon-do, where he excelled. Lucas eventually became a second-degree black belt in Tae-kwon-do. What a big accomplishment!

We brought Lucas back to school at home in second grade. He was a good student, patient and attentive. In the two years since we'd had our initial experience of homeschool, more options for curriculum were published. The history-based one I found used more real books than textbooks and featured a colorful, detailed timeline that spanned two walls.

I was excited to be back to Mom's-hands-on education, and I learned, a little bit better, to allow normal home life to be part of our educational adventures. We found a small but growing group of homeschool families who met in Hall County, Georgia, and we joined in with them. They were a big blessing to us.

"Children are forced to live very rapidly in order to live at all. They are given only a few years in which to learn hundreds of thousands of things about life and the planet and themselves." – Phyllis McGinley, Pulitzer Prizewinning American author (Quote origin: *Sixpence in Her Shoe;* quote found at wonderfulquote.com)

Chapter 19: ISSUES (and Temptation)

We had no second car for several months. Roger had his company car, but when the van we bought was repossessed, the kids and I only had Ben's old Bug available. We learned some hard lessons financially. Our church, Living Water, bailed us out on our mortgage arrears. What a blessing and, at the same time, a very humbling experience!

Pastor Miranda sat down with us and helped us craft a budget. It was amazing how we went from hopeless to encouraged. He came to our house, sacrificing his time to show us that when one cuts out unnecessary spending, gives the Lord a tithe, and prays for wisdom, what is left is enough and the family can make it.

It should have been obvious to us; why did we need somebody to explain 1+1=2? If you have 2 and spend 3, you will be in debt. But the patient instruction Pastor Miranda gave was so helpful. It meant a great deal to us. I'm glad that when we needed help, the church was there.

At first, in my discouragement, I thought,

"So, we stop the newspaper; how is that going to make a difference?"

It absolutely did. Of course, it wasn't just the newspaper. Everything non-essential was cut from our spending. It took us being willing to start learning discipline in the area of finances. Afterward, to see that the money Roger made was enough to pay the bills and put food on the table was such a happy realization! The Lord was there, helping us, showing us that He would sustain our family. There would be enough.

The fact that the church didn't just give advice, they also gave us money for two-months' mortgage arrears and multiple bags of groceries. So sweet! So generous!

We give the Lord thanks for his people. We moved so often, but God led us to fellowship nearly every place we lived. The Lord is faithful—always!

We traveled forty-five minutes one-way every Sunday to get to church. It was an exciting place, where we sang good worship songs and heard the Bible preached. For the first couple of years after we found that church, Pastor Mike Mann led the congregation. Mark Miranda was an elder. However, Pastor Mann was removed when some improprieties were discovered that involved the mishandling of church funds.

M. Miranda became pastor. Before that change in leadership was completed, Roger was dragged into the middle of it. The hassle, the tedious meetings...All of it was disappointing and exhausting.

The church we had moved away from in Reno when coming to the South had also suffered a scandal soon after we left. Inappropriate and sinful behaviors tore through that dear group of saints like a hand grenade going off. The details in Nevada weren't the same as those in Georgia. It was painful for everyone, even for us removed as we were.

In Matthew chapter thirteen, through several parables the Lord points out that there will be good and bad in his kingdom on earth until the end of time. At the time of the end, the angels will separate the good from the bad. Then all will be perfect and good. But until then, we needn't be shocked when bad emerges, even in the church as well as in other places. We live with the coexistence of good and bad, light and dark, wisdom and foolishness.

Thankfully, many scriptures give us directions about how to fix things, how to respond in correcting love, forgiveness, and even with the possibility of restoration for the straying leader or member.

When the fallout settled at Living Water, Pastor Miranda asked us to get to church on time. Roger and I taught Sunday School in turns, and we were chronically a few minutes late for the group prayer before teaching.

On a particular day when we were late again, Pastor Miranda asked us to attend Sunday School but not teach.

Roger had prepared the lesson, and he found that correction offensive. Over that small thing, my husband had us leave the church. He found us another one. This was not something I agreed with, but I did attend where Roger wanted us to go.

The new pastor's name was Johnny. The redundant topic of Johnny's sermons was how much better this church was than other churches in the area. Contrasting that unbiblical, unhelpful content with the scripture-filled messages Pastor Miranda gave made me unhappy. Roger must have been a little upset too, but he acted like he was delighted with every aspect of the new place.

At this new gathering of believers, I experienced an unwelcome temptation with regards to a beautiful man. I didn't know him. I no longer remember his name (thankfully), but the infatuation was strong. This blonde hunk was a young husband and father. I found myself thinking about him. It took prayer and a concerted effort to put him out of my mind.

I realized it was a set-up from the Enemy, a craftily laid trap. But it was such an appealing little pastime. Lustful thoughts landed in my consciousness, and I had to make the choice to push them away; think about somebody else. Lord Jesus, help me! I dealt with this by myself, me and Jesus. I thank the Lord that he provided a way of escape.

First Corinthians 10:13 says, "No temptation has overtaken you that is not common to man. God is faithful, and he will not let you be tempted beyond your ability, but with the temptation he will also provide the way of escape, that you may be able to endure it."

My "way of escape" was prayer to my Father in heaven, coupled with denial of self and repeated, decisive turning away from those thoughts. I found the best ways to push out the offending imaginations were to speak memorized scriptures or prayers or songs. Sing to God! Glorify him and turn away from evil. Filling our hearts and our lips with song is good for us. Ephesians 5:18-19, "...be filled with the Spirit, addressing one another in psalms and hymns and spiritual songs, singing and making melody to the Lord with your heart..."

Paul the apostle confirms that we must fill our minds with good things: "Finally, brothers, whatever is true, whatever is honorable, whatever is just, whatever is pure, whatever is lovely, whatever is commendable, if there is any excellence, if there is anything worthy of praise, think about these things." Philippians 4:8

Say *no* to self. In Luke 9:23-25, Jesus instructs:

..."If anyone would come after me, let him deny himself and take up his cross daily and follow me. For whoever would save his life will lose it, but whoever loses his life for my sake will save it. For what does it profit a man if he gains the whole world and loses or forfeits himself?"

Years later, I encountered this temptation a second time. Interestingly, again I was struggling with Roger. Again, I knew he was wrong about a decision. The second time of this near-headlong fall was like an electric, instant obsession with a man I knew but did not find attractive. Very weird. The mirage seemed so real...Come on! Dana, go for happiness!

It was so strong and constant...in my head I heard,

"Roger and the kids will be fine; his wife and kids will be fine...He and I need to get together!"

So compelling it was, I cannot describe it.

I had to go to my husband, a couple of days later, to confess what was happening inside my spirit, how my thoughts were being hijacked. I asked him to help me...to please watch over me...and to pray for me. Roger eyed me a bit funny and asked if this was something that occurred often. I answered,

"No. And it's not a joke."

Roger did pray and watch over me, and the temptation went away after a couple of months.

Thankfully, temptation is not sin. The Lord taught his disciples and us to pray, "...lead us not into temptation." That's found in Luke 11 and Matthew 6. Help us, Lord Jesus.

If a similar lustful temptation comes to you, please consider:

that heart-pounding interest…maybe it's not "chemistry." Maybe it's a set-up.

Roger had a desk job and was off the route. He had a salary. So, no more commission-only pay. But the job was still stressful. Helping his guys service customers and sell new business was a big responsibility.

After he'd worked as District Manager in Gainesville, Georgia, for four years, an Assistant GM position opened up a couple of hours away, in Charlotte, North Carolina. Roger accepted the work opportunity and went to Charlotte.

For fifteen months, the kids and I stayed in Georgia, doing daily life and trying to sell the house. We saw Roger Friday evenings. He called on the phone and talked to us every night, but our weekends with him were all too brief. Sunday night or early Monday morning, he had to leave for work and for his hotel room again.

Many families make sacrifices so that the husband or wife can attend college classes or do postgraduate work. Roger educated himself, taking opportunities for advancement in his field of service, sales, and management in the real world by willingly relocating to where opportunities appeared. We sacrificed time with him so that he could take these chances. I admire Roger's gutsy perseverance and his desire to learn and to work hard.

In addition to Roger's diligent hard work though, something else was going on in my husband…something I could not identify. As the weeks and months of his work in Charlotte dragged on, I felt that the Lord had a hand in removing Roger from our home. I sensed we were better off without his daily presence. I didn't know all the reasons, but I became satisfied to be faithful to my responsibilities. I could wait and trust God. He was at work in Roger and in me.

I recommend an article from *Public Discourse*: "Your Marriage: You Have No Idea of the Good You are Doing," by Doug Mainwaring. Please read it.

Also, a book: Ryan Anderson describes and defends the institution of marriage, which all people in all cultures have known about forever. Until 2000. He says that defining marriage is rather like explaining why wheels are round. Good book. (Note [xvi])

Chapter 20: God Guides

Busy as life was, I volunteered for a Crisis Pregnancy Center in Gainesville, Georgia, a couple of times a week when I could get there. Or I took my turn answering the phone remotely for them when the office was closed.

As I mentioned, Ella and I had a difficult relationship when she was in her teens. She was a great kid: beautiful, funny, engaging (with others), a great student, and a good babysitter for her younger siblings. I was trying to be a good and faithful mom, but, especially during this season, we clashed whenever we got within ten feet of each other.

When a child's spirit closes to a parent, measures must be discovered and initiated to invite the child out of that shell. But I didn't know how to make the prickly exterior smooth out. These difficulties lasted until Ella was nineteen or twenty. Growing up helped. But there were other factors too, like my clumsy parenting, and like me trying to do it all myself, failing to ask Roger for help.

Imperfect as we parents are, yet God gives grace. How faithful God is! And he constantly teaches us more about faithfulness too. (Note [xvii])

Ella and Ben's birth-dad came to Georgia for Ben's high school graduation. A few months after that brief visit, Ella appealed to us; she wanted to go live with her dad.

We were trying to sell the house and move to North Carolina. So, big upheavals were coming soon for all of us. I asked Roger what he thought about Ella's request. He stated that it was okay with him. No discussion. He didn't bat it around at all, just said that it was a good idea. Ella could go live with her dad. In California. Clear across the country. That surprised me. I was counting on him saying, "No."

Ella asked the school counselor at East Hall for her opinion. She conveyed also that it would be good.

We told our Ella, "We'll let you go."

Inside, I was so sad; I felt that this was not a good thing. Though Mr. Babb was presently on an even keel, I didn't know how stable he really was. He and his third wife had parted ways. Ella was excited. Mr. Babb was buying furniture for his extra bedroom so he could have a special, welcoming home for Ella.

Not knowing exactly why my world quaked and heaved, our decision hung over me. I was burdened and tearful in my prayer times. I went to Roger and told him how unhappy I felt about sending my girl away. I asked if we could revisit the decision or get counsel from the Mirandas.

He admitted that he didn't really think it would be good for Ella to go. "But," he continued, "I said what I did because you never listen to me anyway. And, no. Do not go to our former pastor for counsel."

Wow! I was trying out this submitting thing, and this is what it got me? A thoughtless brush-off instead of husbandly counsel.

Honestly, it was a new thing for me to regard Roger as my authority in the Lord. It's not surprising that he didn't expect me to pay any attention to his words.

The bottom line, though, was that Roger had withheld from me his true opinion. And we'd taken the secular, off-the-cuff advice from the high school counselor.

Then I clearly "heard" a Scripture verse in my heart. It was from Psalm 1; a Bible chapter Mom had us kids memorize when I was five years old.

It begins this way, "Blessed is the man who walks not in the counsel of the ungodly…" (NKJV)

That was it. This school counselor fit the description exactly. She was ungodly. A couple of years before, she had blocked the Crisis Pregnancy Center from getting a good, proven, abstinence-based sex ed curriculum into East Hall High School.

I suddenly knew that Roger and I needed to back the whole decision up, do an about face. I figured the resulting fireworks might burn the whole house down. So, I needed confirmation, wisdom, and lots of prayer.

I couldn't go to that new preacher, Pastor Johnny, for counsel. I picked up the phone and called our old pastor and asked if I could come over. He and his dear wife were still gracious friends. They would pray for us and help me pray for Ella. I was so afraid she would get hurt by this big move. Though Roger didn't want me to ask for counsel from the Mirandas, I had to have prayer. They did listen to me; they did pray. I can still hear Pastor Miranda's deep voice interceding, "Gloria, gloria, gloria…"

I went back home after visiting our former pastor and explained to Roger that I wanted to go with what he really believed, and what I thought was right. We needed to back track. Ella needed to wait until she was older to move to California to be with her dad. Roger agreed! Wow.

In a relieved shiver, I almost literally heard the beep, beep, beep warning of a big vehicle backing up. (Note [xviii])

"To keep your marriage brimming, With love in the loving cup,

Whenever you're wrong, admit it; Whenever you're right, shut up." – Ogden Nash, American humorist (Found at brainyquotes.com., accessed 4/25/2022)

Chapter 21: God Provides. Chicks Fly.

Unbelievably, maybe miraculously, Ella accepted our decision.

She didn't freak out or blow up or run away. That had been my biggest fear throughout those months, that she might run away. Thank the Lord for guarding our girl—and for leading our family in his path.

Roger's promotion and move came in the fall of Ben's senior year, so the first autumn he was gone to Charlotte without us was the fall of 1989. But, that last year of Ben's high school, before Roger left for that new job, he did get to go to most of those important football games to see our Ben, our linebacker, block. Roger, and all of us, loved cheering loudly at those games.

My husband stayed in hotels during the week. The kids and I didn't go see him in Charlotte. Busy with school and life, we could barely keep up while taking care of meals, laundry, running errands, getting the teenagers to and from where they needed to go, Lucas to Karate lessons, Jayna and Lucas to homeschool get-togethers, all while enjoying our happy toddler.

We endlessly ran all over our part of Hall County, despite not always having dependable transportation. The five children and I lived out in the boonies, sometimes with only Ben's ancient, beat up, orange Bug to get us where we needed to go. And that thing had to be rolled off a hill, popping the clutch to make it start.

About a year into this separate life, Roger began to worry me a little bit by telling stories about some woman. She reminded him of a character actress we admired. He even said, "She is way more like me than you are, Dana."

The Lord protected my man, shepherding him through this trial he seemed almost oblivious to.

Roger had lost his wedding band years before. I didn't like it that he wore nothing on his ring finger.

When he worked nearby it was less an issue. But Roger dismissed the missing ring as completely unimportant. He wasn't going to worry about buying a wedding ring when there were so many other demands on his paycheck.

I bought my husband an inexpensive, sterling silver ring, and he put it on. He was surprised that a waitress at a restaurant he frequented noticed and congratulated him on his marriage. Roger, confused, replied that he'd been married for ten years. He told me that story as though it were unbelievable. Cluelessness, it turns out, can affect Roger too.

He realized it was time for him to find us a house, and within two weeks he found a good rental near Charlotte. But before we moved, that woman made a big play for my Roger. She came to his room, and he confessed to me that he ended up almost falling into a trap. Thankfully, he recognized it and escaped her ruse.

Roger told me the story but proceeded to act like it was no big deal. Hey! I wanted some dust-and-ashes-type repentance on his part. It bothered me that he let himself be drawn that far into a dangerous web. But he did realize the danger. And the fact that he talked to me about what happened when it was a fresh victory over temptation signaled a new openness between us. I thanked the Lord.

The move that got our family back into one location came after Ben headed to college. He was a great student and hard worker, getting the highest SAT score among those graduating from East Hall High School his senior year. At the graduation ceremony he was honored as co-Salutatorian, and he offered the prayer at the ceremony.

Our son was accepted at both colleges he applied to—one large and one small—and was awarded scholarships to both. He decided to attend the smaller college, a military school in north Georgia that offered him the larger scholarship.

Ben was excited about getting out on his own, and I didn't worry too much about my son. The Lord is faithful. I can trust him to care for my kids, wherever they are.

Ben was living on campus in the middle of his freshman year in Dahlonega, ("Duh-LON-e-guh") Georgia, when we left our Lula, Georgia, house sitting empty.

We headed to North Carolina to rejoin Roger.

So, we had one child in college in Georgia and four with us in North Carolina. It was the right thing for us to move and get our family back together. It had to happen if Roger and I were to stay married. But the new house was short one bedroom. There was no good place for Ben to squeeze in. After a year, when Ben decided the military school wasn't a good fit for him, he moved to California to be with his dad. Ben planned to further his education out west. Thus, our oldest chick flew from the nest.

For Ella, our move to North Carolina came midway through her eleventh-grade classes, a trying time to uproot. That summer, when Ben moved, she took some months off and drove west with him. She visited their dad and other family, applying to a couple of colleges before she left. Surprisingly, she wasn't only accepted, but also won a great scholarship to an exclusive, private college near us. At age sixteen!

Ella lived at home and worked hard at all her studies that first year. Also working a part-time job, she still made good grades. When her gift shop job at the nearby mall ended, our daughter went to work part-time with Roger. She helped in the office at Aramark in Charlotte. Seeing up close the level of responsibility Roger had at work and how much people relied on him gave Ella a new respect for him.

A move onto campus made sense when school started up again and Ella got more involved in social aspects of college life. We watched her change and grow. In high school, Ella had often worn her hair long and curled. The super-feminine era caught Ella up in waves of hair spray and make up. Then college styles grunged our girl totally when she didn't have to dress carefully, like for work.

After a couple more semesters Ella put college on hold and followed Ben to California. So, our nest continued to shrink. I felt there was something important about the relationships out West, so far from me. Though it hurt my heart to let go, the Lord was at work. He knows how to cover and care for our kids. Always.

That one-bedroom-short North Carolina house was the first of three in the Charlotte area. In the second one, God answered a specific prayer of mine and provided for us in a remarkable way. Here's the story:

The house was laid out in a huge open floor plan, and I was concerned about the power bill. What would it cost over the winter? There were two fireplaces. So, I prayed that the Lord would provide firewood. A day or two later, workmen for Duke Power knocked on the front door asking permission to take down a large dead tree on the land. I tried to refer them to the owner, but they assured me that I could give permission as a renter. So, I agreed.

The wood from that big tree was already cured perfectly as it had been dead for some time. I was amazed and humbled—and so excited! I'd cried out to the Lord of heaven and earth, and he'd heard me! God hired three men to work at cutting wood for us for three days. They not only cut the tree down, but they also sawed it up and split it into lengths that fit into the fireplaces.

I cried tears of joy and gratefulness over that firewood, feeling the Lord's everlasting arms around me. This was concrete (or wooden) evidence of our Father's care for me. For us. He is so faithful.

The third house in that area was one we had an opportunity to buy. The outside of the house boasted shade and more shade. There were more than fifty trees on our corner lot. It was almost impossible to grow grass there, but two or three beautiful, established azalea bushes grew beside the front walk.

It was an older split-level brick house. We scraped off the old wallpaper and cleaned or removed carpet. We found hardwood floors. I followed Roger's new, clean paint with my own homemade stencils in pretty Shaker-type patterns in muted browns and blues. We updated the kitchen cabinets, painting them bright white while jarring our senses with wide stripes of navy and white wallpaper. I loved it.

My favorite thing was a living room that fit our piano on one level and a den/TV room downstairs. Two separate living areas! Anyone could still hear the other area, but not necessarily be rubbing shoulders with all the family all the time.

We discovered Christian neighbors who also homeschooled their children, and we became friends. We settled there for a few years.

We'd found a church while in the second Charlotte-area house. It was a vibrant new fellowship that met in a theater. The senior pastor, Brad, preached the Word of God. Families there seemed to have their kids in order in an attractive, happy way we hadn't seen before. Associate pastor, Robert, led worship with God-honoring skill. They were lovely, friendly folks, and they welcomed us into fellowship.

Two of our kids had some learning or perception differences and fine motor skills problems. Homeschool was a great way to gear lessons to their specific needs. The Lord sent us resources and friendship by providing testing and encouragement through Mary, a new friend we found at church. She had multiple degrees in evaluating and teaching children with learning differences, and she generously helped us.

After testing them, Mary encouraged us that the English and early reading curriculum I'd been using was probably the only one on the market that would have worked for teaching our kids to read. She rejoiced with us that the Lord had provided so well. She also pointed us toward other helpful, good curriculums and showed us lots of strategies for teaching and learning. What a blessing Mary was to us!

Book recommendation:

Sixpence in Her Shoe by Phyllis McGinley, Pulitzer Prizewinning American author (1905-1978) Mrs. McGinley wrote appreciatively of the roles of wife, mother, and homemaker in a time when feminists loudly denounced and shamed women who found fulfillment in traditional roles in their homes. Mrs. McGinley, old-fashioned and lady-like, lived and wrote in a different era, a time when parks were filled with children and more women reared their own kids. She was funny and wise. Her chapter, "How Not to Kill Your Husband," is worth the price of the book. Search through old book sites and find it!

Chapter 22: Our Nest Expands

Roger worked lots of hours. The kids were growing. Life was busy. So, why not add foster care to our schedule? One bright Sunday morning, a woman stood up in church and challenged us in the congregation to become foster parents. The agency she worked for needed homes that would provide temporary placements for infants.

Jayna, our ten-year-old daughter, asked if we could help. "Could we take care of a baby? Could we do foster care?"

We agreed. "Sure. Why not? If a baby needs a place to stay for a while, they can certainly stay with us."

We started the process and got licensed to do foster care in Mecklenburg County.

That year, 1994, was stressful for Roger and me. I was becoming overwhelmed. I felt like all the responsibility for the kids and the bills weighed on me. That was unfair because Roger worked hard to earn the money. He put in long hours at work, committing himself to the success of his company and his customers. Additionally, he loved taking his turn one time each month teaching ten-year-olds their Sunday School lessons. We hosted a Care Group at our house mid-week, though sometimes Roger didn't make it to that meeting.

A burdening grief added a worrisome, sad background to life for Roger and all of us. His mother's health was failing. Grandma Dorothy was drawing near to the end of her earthly days.

Meanwhile, Ben had been in California for two years. In that time, he'd made his way back and forth to see us a couple of times, but we hadn't visited him. We knew he was no longer living with his dad. He had tried renting with a few guys, which didn't last long. Now he was living with his girlfriend. Roger and I made a plan for me to go see Ben and his girlfriend and Ella too, who'd moved there recently. I'd go the middle of August.

In July we got a call from the adoption agency. Did we want to take a new baby girl? Yes! We were ready to begin our foster care journey. We dug out our old highchair and borrowed a cradle. Jayna and I went to the store, bought a diaper bag and a newborn-size dress in a pretty, purple print. Then we drove the five miles to the agency office and waited. And waited. They didn't come. After an hour, we found a pay phone and called them.

"Oh. Sorry. The birth mom changed her mind and is keeping her baby."

We were glad for the baby, but disappointed for us. We shed some tears driving back home. Little did we know that another baby girl was being born that day who would become very important to us. The Lord was saving her place in that cradle in Roger's and my bedroom.

Two days later we got the call: "Do you still want a baby girl?"

"Great! Yes, we want her!"

This time the person from the agency brought the little foster baby to our house straight from the hospital. I had to run Lucas to his Tae-kwon-do class a couple of blocks away that rainy day, and hurry as I might, the woman from the agency beat me, getting the baby to our home a few minutes before I arrived.

There the beautiful baby was, in her little car seat on the kitchen table, when Barnabas and I walked into the house. We called her Gracie, and we were instantly hooked on this perfect, blonde, brown-eyed little one.

Barnabas was seven, so it had been that long since we'd dealt with long-term, newborn-focused sleep-deprivation. The nap-when-you-can lifestyle returned with a yawn, a baby on one hip, and the kids and dog in tow. We loved caring for little Grace. And church friends and work friends and family were excited with us that we had her in our home. Roger's mom was very sick, but she was happy for us too.

Dorothy passed away in August. What sad news! It was a blow, a first terrible brush with death for all the kids. Grandma Dorothy had put up a grand battle against the last enemy.

I felt relief for her. She was no longer sick. She suffered no more and was now with the Lord. But seeing Roger and the children grieve... It was difficult.

Funny how life goes from this to that: birth to death, grief to hope. We decided we wouldn't change the ticket we had bought for me to go see our big kids. I flew to California to see our Ben and Ella, and to meet Ben's girlfriend, Lynn. The kids made me very comfortable. Ben worked and surfed and took time to show me his favorite beaches up and down their part of the coast. I talked about the importance of marriage and about them following the Lord's rule in life. They listened. Soon after I got back home to North Carolina, Ben called to say they were planning a wedding for the next spring.

While we were in Georgia for Dorothy's funeral, and then while I was in California, the agency found us respite care for our foster baby. I was anxious to get her back when I returned. Grace was only away from us a week and a half, but we missed her.

Over that year, 1994-1995, we welcomed five foster babies. We called them: Grace, Brooke, Charlie, Dillon, and Eleanor. It was a busy year, some of the time having two little guest babies at the same time in our home and our hearts.

That fall, in the middle of our foster care adventure, God put me and Roger on the same team, united like we'd never been before. But first, we nearly ended this marriage of ours once again.

"Whoever thinks marriage is a fifty-fifty proposition doesn't know the half of it." – Franklin P. Jones, American reporter and public relations executive

Chapter 23: Marriage Problems After Fourteen Years

Heading into our forties, we'd grown apart somehow. Roger and I lived separate, busy, totally different experiences of life. With that divergence, neither of us appreciated what was going on with our mate.

Roger had started lashing out in spurts, raging in huge blow-ups every three to six months. These explosions were short-lived but damaging. My husband's focus, his whole trajectory, was living and breathing his work. Grappling with deadlines and people issues, customers, accounts payable, route guys, equipment failures, contests, hiring and firing while trying to satisfy multiple, impossible bosses—these were just a few challenges Roger faced. He used nearly all his gifts during fifty-plus hours a week at work.

Depositing his weekly paycheck into our joint checking account, Roger trusted me to manage the finances and all the rest. I worked non-stop at our home, doing (or supervising) dishes and laundry, writing checks for the bills, homeschooling, etc.

I felt unappreciated. And I was angry, but, strange to say, I did not know it. I felt no qualms looking at my husband as a hypocrite who loudly sang worship songs on Sunday but didn't act the perfect Christian around the house the rest of the week. Ungodly comparison is warned of in 2 Corinthians 10:12:

"For we dare not class ourselves or compare ourselves with those who commend themselves. But they, measuring themselves by themselves, and comparing themselves among themselves, are not wise." (NKJV)

I did commend myself. I felt that I was a godly woman going about my life pretty much as well as anyone could. Roger was the problem. Not me.

Roger and I got into a big fight when he man-handled the boys. I don't remember what Lucas and Barnabas had done, but I know I did not like how Roger was dealing with them. I tried to intervene, and then Roger and I got into it. This happened in front of two of the neighbor kids who were playing at our house. It was terrible and completely embarrassing.

Looking back, I believe that detail about our friends' children being there and running home crying, was evidence of God's grace. We'd been keeping our anger problems in the dark. But the Lord was beginning his rescue. He shone in on a dim corner where that anger of ours hid.

Burning embers of dissatisfaction, self-righteousness, and ungodly comparison smoldered in my heart, not to mention a lack of respect for my husband. (See Ephesians 5:33) These sins needed to be raked out, scattered, and stepped on. All that was about to happen. Because the neighbor kids were present, we were forced to view this family fight differently than previous ones. It had been dragged out into the light.

Things settled down after the altercation. Roger and I made our way across the street to apologize to the neighbors for losing our cool and scaring their kids.

Late that night I sat down to write out my feelings. Writing might help me work through the chaos churning inside of me. I had a couple of little notebooks I journaled in from time to time. Finding one from three months before, I opened it up. The last entry reminded me of Roger's really bad Father's Day…a shameful, angry day.

I was shocked that, there on that page, the thoughts swirling and stuttering through my mind were already written down in black and white. We'd done this exact same thing a few months earlier. It bothered me that I had forgotten. Yet, I thought maybe it was good. Maybe that was what true forgiveness looked like. Maybe I really was wonderful and forgiving. Maybe I was the holy, righteous, longsuffering one. And Roger was the ogre. I let tears flow.

Roger was asleep, and that wasn't unusual. He had to go to work early, so he was always asleep way before me. And he usually was up and gone before I awakened. With the new baby guest, though, I woke up at odd times.

So, the next morning, I went downstairs to find him before he left, which, in retrospect, was stupid. He always hated to be slowed down when he had to get out the door...even on a good day when there was a good word on my lips. This was not a good day. But I needed to try to sort out the aftermath. I wasn't okay.

It was one of those times when I knew what would happen. If I say this, he will say that. But I couldn't ignore it. I had to try. Roger shrugged, "What aftermath?"

I accused, "What do you mean, 'what aftermath?'"

Then he reacted, letting his anger flare at me. I knew he would. But he went further than usual, fuming that there was no reason to stay. He was going to find an apartment and move out.

"And don't call the church. If you do, I'm not going to them for marriage counseling."

I remember thinking, "I've done this single-parent thing. It was a long time ago, but I guess I can do it again."

A song that sustained me during that time was one by Twila Paris. The music video for it was a pretty, artistic, Monet-brushed thing. I watched and listened and cried as she sang of God being in control of all things, managing and fixing all the details of life, not forsaking us, his children.

I called Robert, our associate pastor, music minister, youth leader, and counseling pastor. I needed to make an appointment. Looking over old calendars and journals, I am surprised by the actual timeline.

I remembered the main things accurately, but I thought we got in to see Pastor Robert for counseling more quickly than we did. Life went on. And death. My little sister died unexpectedly in early November. I flew to Nevada for the memorial service for Carol. The foster care people allowed me to take baby Grace along that time.

"The difference between courtship and marriage is the difference between the pictures in the seed catalog and what comes up." – James Wharton, American writer (Quote taken from *Worth Repeating* © Copyright 2003 by Bob Kelly. Published by Kregel Publications, Grand Rapids, MI. Used by permission of the publisher. All rights reserved.)

Chapter 24: Greetings With Kisses

The first counseling appointment with Pastor Robert was in late November that year. Roger did come along. The bottom line of Robert's counsel was,

"Read the Bible and do what it says."

This would be a timely rescue because we'd been treating each other as if the Bible instructed,

"Husbands, mock your wives; wives, belittle your husbands."

When we walked into the office, Pastor Robert said,

"Other counselors will tell you, 'It took you years to get this messed up; it will take years to unravel everything.' But I don't have years. I have four weeks."

He continued, "But the background information you have given me also indicates that, if you don't take immediate steps to turn your marriage around, you won't stay married for long."

Wow. We had better pay attention.

Pastor Robert then started with me…by addressing my anger. I wanted to deflect that focus, saying, "Hey, I'm not the one who was throwing the kids around!"

But there was an awareness again, like I'd had when listening to counselor Bill D. thirteen or fourteen years earlier. I trusted that this was God's counsel. This was the Lord's rescue cable thrown to me. I drop it at my own and my family's peril. So, though it was uncomfortable, I sat there and paid attention. Later, I found out that our pastor was following the biblical pattern of addressing the one under authority first, then the one in authority. See Ephesians five, verses 22-23.

I hated what was revealed when Pastor Robert started kicking around in the ash heap of my heart. There definitely was a lurking anger. I'd been sowing at least as much discord into our home as Roger had. Here, I thought of myself as the abused, put-upon, godly one. I'd thought,

"If only Roger, or the kids, (or whoever) could get it together, we'd be fine."

Not true. Now that I could see it, it was unbelievable that I'd been blind to it before. I had been groping, fuming, and stumbling like someone born with no senses. Deceived and deafened by my own sin, I didn't even know the anger in me (and erupting out toward them) was doing such huge damage to Roger and the kids.

When I'd let my anger or theirs stymie our relationship, I had failed. Instead of figuring out how to make our home a place of peace, I'd been self-focused, perceiving myself a victim. And not a quiet victim…I often yelled and slammed around the house, so angry and discontented.

The shock I felt when the Lord gave me insight, to see that sinful anger, my sin of defensive wrath…it is hard to describe. God let me observe something in the spiritual realm that was really ugly.

I was devastated. The few tears I let myself shed were not ones of self-pity but of horrified, surprised realization. The naked truth was that I was a vengeful woman. Unapproachable. Scary. Not righteous.

God is transforming me, but I am right only where clothed in the righteousness of Jesus our perfect, loving Master. (1 Corinthians 1:26-31)

Later I experienced gratefulness that the Lord does not show us all our sins at once. It is a difficult thing to face, a "revolting development"—a phrase my dad used. I really was revolted at what the Lord showed me in my heart.

Humbled, I repented and prayed to turn from the sin of anger.

Repentance is cleansing! It's like a good scrub. The Lord Jesus taught his disciples to pray,

"… forgive us our debts, as we also have forgiven our debtors. And lead us not into temptation, but deliver us from evil." Matthew 6:12-13

The daily washing of repentance is needful. We need to pray for forgiveness regularly like we need to bathe. Dr. Ed Young's daily devotional called "Everywhere I Go: Learning to See Jesus" includes a helpful article on repentance and forgiveness. (Note [xix])

I began to realize that if and when I ever see my own sin such that I turn and repent, it is the grace of God working in me. I don't remember the particulars of Pastor Robert's words to me, but the gist is stamped indelibly on my mind. I had a big responsibility to set the tone in our home. I'd been setting it, all right. Not in a good way.

Thankfully, the Lord immediately began to cleanse away the anger that had been distracting and poisoning me and hurting our marriage. And by God's grace I was comforted and encouraged to move forward.

Pastor Robert's first homework assignment was to write out ten things we liked about our spouse before we met with him again. Being at the very beginning of what the Lord was doing to rescue us, I as yet had no warm feelings toward my husband. I stared at the blank page, unable to come up with anything positive to say about Roger. I must've eventually thought of something to write down, describing the good man and provider my husband was—and is. I'm too much of a teacher-pleasing, *A student* to head back to class without my homework finished.

I believe it was the next week that our homework was to read all five chapters of the epistle of First Peter every day.

"Read the Bible and do what it says."

I did read it through two or three times that week. The directive to wives in 1 Peter 3 follows instructions to servants in Chapter 2 and begins, "Likewise…"

Wives? Likewise? The same as servants? Nice—not! I don't think I like that very much, Mr. Peter-the-Apostle. (Note [xx])

Yet, God's word to servants follows instructions to citizens subject to national rule (that of the not-always-perfect-emperor) and of local governmental authorities: "Live as people who are free...living as servants of God." 1 Peter 2:16

God notices everything! He is proud of us when we follow him and do well; he is patient (or maybe not, depending on how many times he's let us slide...!) when we mess up.

I read and reread First Peter. There was the part in Chapter 3 that talks about God being pleased when we endure suffering for righteousness' sake. "That's me," I thought. "That's me!"

Wait! "Do it with gentleness and respect?" I didn't think Roger or any of my kids would describe me as "gentle" or "respectful" very often. Sigh! Lord Jesus, help me.

Peter's letter is such a precious part of the Bible. In it I found this: "...casting all your anxieties on him, because he cares for you." 1 Peter 5:7. What a treasured verse!

But the part of First Peter that turned our marriage around was the ending. The last verse says, "Greet one another with the kiss of love..."

It struck me that I was to greet Roger. That verse rang in my ears like a loud church bell. Greet him with a kiss. I hadn't been greeting him at all. I barely grunted when my Roger came home. But if folks at the churches Peter wrote to were to greet each other, there at the meetings, greet with a kiss...? Okay – read the Bible; do what it says.

I treated it like a recipe. Hear him coming in the door. Rise. Go to my husband. Say "hello." Give him a perfunctory kiss.

It was not a real heart-felt thing at first. But it was one of those small acts of obedience to the Lord that God took and turned into something he could use.

This simple exercise got us off the treadmill of boring sameness and unpleasant predictability. Instead of thinking, "I already know everything about you. You'll never change," we began to love one another. We had a marriage!

Our life together was no longer a barely joint endeavor, but something that gave us hope. We found that our home could be lovely and safe. Roger responded and softened toward me immediately; he did not notice that I was initially following a "recipe."

Soon we were on the same side, the same team! Anger was retreating. Pastor Robert was right; it only took four weeks, maybe less! I would've never believed it if I'd not lived it. Our awesome God is fabulous and amazing!

"A happy marriage is the union of two good forgivers." – Ruth Graham, American author. (AZQuotes.com, Wind and Fly LTD, 2022. https://www.azquotes.com/quote/515851, accessed April 20, 2022.)

Chapter 25: NC to MD

Grace, our first foster baby, stayed with us for eight months. At that point the agency placed her with a family who planned to adopt her. We missed our baby girl and prayed daily for her. But I was able to look at the empty place left in our home as something we'd signed up to do. We were her foster family, after all.

Roger and the kids just couldn't let Gracie go. They prayed hard for her, and she definitely needed those prayers. We found out later that she cried inconsolably and was so distraught, that the family she was with wondered if something major was wrong. Lucas, our fourteen-year-old, teased that he'd told her to do that so that we would get her back.

The social worker called to ask if we had noticed problems with the baby.

"No. There was nothing wrong with Gracie. She was fine. Perfect. She was smart and loving and coordinated, nearly walking at eight months." That was just before she left our home.

We started praying harder and told the agency that if Grace needed us, we wanted her. We'd love to adopt her.

The placement with the other family failed. They backed out of the adoption.

One fine summer day, the kids and I had just gotten back from swimming with friends when the phone rang. The social worker told me of the other family's decision and asked if we still wanted Grace.

"Yes!"

I had Lucas, Jayna, and Barnabas sit down on the couch before I tried to page Roger. I asked the kids, "What would you want if you could ask for anything right now?"

They answered, "Anything? We'd want Gracie back!"

When the phone call came, Roger was at a car dealer, looking to find a new car for work. I paged him. He called me back and welcomed the news with a "Glory! Hallelujah!"

Yay! The Lord gave us our little girl back for keeps.

Roger had just accepted a job in Baltimore, nine hours away, to work as General Manager at another textile company. He had that day given a month's notice to the job in Charlotte.

Our move from North Carolina to Maryland certainly seemed like it was going to be easy. A piece of cake! We'd even visited a Maryland church related to the one in Charlotte that we loved so much. There we found the same type of worship and fellowship we'd grown to love, and we felt that was confirmation from the Lord that we were on the right track. And Roger's new company hired movers for us. Wow!

I graphed the rooms and large pieces of furniture, figuring out on paper where things would fit. We could, thus, direct the movers where to place the furniture. Sounded simple.

Even when they should be easy, moves can discomfort and get us lost. Somehow, after boxes were unpacked, I felt troubled and unsettled. It was spring 1996. I was finishing up our homeschooling for the year with Lucas in ninth grade, Jayna in sixth, Barnabas in third. We had adopted Grace, who was now nearly two. She ran around and climbed on us while we worked. Homeschooling is busy but not overwhelming. Strangely, the thought kept recurring that I was too close to Pennsylvania...

I wasn't okay. Something felt strange, like I was teetering on the verge of some kind of breakdown.

When I was seven, Dad moved our family from Nevada to Pennsylvania. He wanted to live near where he'd grown up. For one year we lived in a row house in York, Pennsylvania. Then we moved twelve miles out of town to a big, old, drafty, brick farmhouse beside Lake Pahagaco.

Pennsylvania held bad memories for me. Daddy had many times made our home a terrifying place. He'd been faithful in one important area—he continued to read the Bible to us daily—but Dad spanked hard with the belt.

He clenched his big, right hand into a fist and bit his lip, giving my brothers "lickings." They got them more often than I did, but I ended up the most fearful, I think.

Mom, our wise and loving comforter, taught me many Bible verses to counteract fear when I awoke from nightmares. Here are two of my favorite fear-fighting scriptures:

"So do not fear, for I am with you; do not be dismayed, for I am your God. I will strengthen you and help you; I will uphold you with my righteous right hand." Isaiah 41:10 (NIV)

"For God has not given us a spirit of fear, but of power and of love and of a sound mind." 2 Timothy 1:7 (NKJV)

I really thought I'd forgiven my dad for things he had done in anger and selfishness. (Note [xxi]) But living only an hour away from my old home in Spring Grove, Pennsylvania, was unnerving me. I prayed for help to feel settled. I asked the Lord for help to forgive Dad who had passed away in 1986. And I prayed for the Lord to release me from Dad's authoritarian ways in some deeper measure. I asked for grace and stability. Still, I struggled.

I don't think my family knew that I was having problems, but I was going into our bedroom, closing the door, and screaming into my pillow at times throughout the day to try to relieve the stress.

I believe that the Lord gives strength for my day (Deuteronomy 33:25). So, I thought I must have been taking on something that wasn't my responsibility to be so fragile and frazzled.

I decided to talk to Roger about taking some responsibilities from me, specifically that he would either take over the responsibility of paying the bills or that he would put Lucas—our dear, sweet, fifteen-year-old—into the private school affiliated with our new church, Estuary Community. This tall, dark-haired, handsome boy was a pretty easy teenager. He loved God, played guitar and sang, was a good brother to the girls and most of the time to Barnabas too. (Brothers love to hassle each other...)

I expected my man to minimize the problem saying,

"Dana, you're fine. You do a great job."

So, before speaking to Roger, I asked the Lord to please help him truly hear me. The Lord answered my prayer. Roger listened.

When I took my troubles to my husband, he did hear me. He agreed to begin writing the checks (and he did a great job managing our finances for a long time.)

Also, he started the process to enroll Lucas in our church school that fall. Not only that, but he also ended up putting Jayna into school, something I was not in favor of at first. But Roger knew best, and I began to experience peace in my life again. Thank God!

In the new season of our marriage since counseling with Pastor Robert, Roger became a good leader, as great a leader in our home as he was at work!

Though I still was a little hesitant to allow Roger to take the reins of our family, it became obvious, even to me, that he had an anointing to lead us that I didn't have. I submitted to my husband in practical ways, and each of us became better and stronger.

"Story writers say that love is concerned only with young people, and the excitement and glamour of romance end at the altar. How blind they are. The best romance is inside marriage; the finest love stories come after the wedding, not before." – Irving Stone, American writer

Chapter 26: Churchville Was Home

We lived in Churchville for eleven years, a record for us. Our cute Cape Cod house was situated on a grassy half-acre lot that also included five or six mature trees.

Many stories could be told of that part of our lives. I homeschooled some of the years there. For a while, I taught English and Writing and Language Arts and Spelling at our church's high school. Then I brought our two youngest home for school again when our sweet Barnabas was expelled half-way through tenth grade.

We had great neighbors. One of those families taught us to garden. They helped us make flower beds in front of the house and on the side. I also made a pretty, concrete sidewalk out to the shed in the back.

We were living there on September 11, 2001. The church school was finishing up a remodel that year. So, the kids weren't yet back to class. I was still teaching, and Barnabas and Gracie were still enrolled. On that beautiful Tuesday morning we were home.

(Lucas was in his own apartment by then, working at his job assisting an engineer while going to college near us.)

Two of Jayna's friends had spent the night. Roger was gone to work; I was listening to the radio, lazing around in my pajamas on the sunny side porch when I heard about the first plane hitting one of the Twin Towers of the World Trade Center in New York City. I pictured a small plane.

Gracie was listening with me, but she wasn't concerned, as I was not yet too worried about this news. I went back inside as Jayna came downstairs. When I told Jayna about the plane, she immediately said,

"Mom, turn on the TV."

I did. Right after we began watching, the second airliner hit. We knew right then that the planes-turned-massive-bombs were no accident. Some evil had done it purposely. So, Grace and Jayna and Jayna's two girlfriends and I watched and rewatched. Barnabas watched a few times than went to skateboard on our driveway.

It finally sank into my horrified consciousness that, especially for Gracie who was seven, those dreadful crashes were perceived as happening again and again every time the coverage was replayed.

Nine-eleven was a terrifying day. But the crashes were limited to four. The terrible, searing images, three fiery crash sites plus that rumpled, Pennsylvania field…The quartet of passenger jets went down while many victims of terrorism died in the planes and on the ground. But thank God, there were not dozens or scores of attacks. We finally turned it off.

Land and air travel were shut down for several days. Two miles away, Interstate 95 eerily sat empty. Silent. Somber flags hung at half-staff.

Then the fearful quiet that had hemmed us in receded as President George W. Bush told us to get back to work. Get back to shopping. To me that sounded wrong at first. But he was right. President Bush knew that if we stayed inside any longer, the terrorists would've achieved their goal.

Patriotic red, white, and blue started appearing everywhere. Along highway 95, overpasses were decorated with large and small American flags.

We still feared more airline attacks and the threatened use of bioweapons. There were many dismaying reasons to stay away from people, but following President Bush's advice, we returned to normal life in the US fairly quickly.

Our country stood against that enemy, teaming together with other nations to fight radical Islamic terrorists in Afghanistan and other places. It was a very different kind of war than we'd faced before. Not only did they attack and kill our civilians, the brutal, militant terrorists often hid behind their own children, families and businesspeople.

Though we grieved the loss of the 3,000 victims of terrorism who died that day, and though some things changed forever with 9/11...Though we were a little less optimistic as a country, God gave courage. He was our help and our shield even in those times where hopes were diminished, and we started to see some of our freedoms eroded.

One place in the Bible where the Lord is called our help and our shield is Psalm 33, especially verse 20-22,

"Our soul waits for the LORD; he is our help and our shield.

For our heart is glad in him, because we trust in his holy name.

Let your steadfast love, O LORD, be upon us, even as we hope in you."

The Lord's care surrounded us through the bad and the good.

Part of the good was that our house was situated across from a sod farm, a great open, green place. In the middle of that sod farm was a big, old, two-story home where a sweet teen-ager lived with her family. Brea welcomed us to the neighborhood with her friendly smile. When the weather turned cold, she often came by for a cup of hot chocolate. Brea came to trust in the Lord Jesus at our house one day, and then she joined us at our church.

Another series of stories and favorite memories from our Churchville years involved a photography business that Roger and I started. We called it Photo by Roger Studios. We shot portraits and events, mostly weddings. Many of our couples were young people from church. Our children were growing up, and some of them got married too while we lived there. Lucas met his bride at Estuary Community Church. Jayna met her groom when she went away from our Churchville home to Bible college in Greenville, South Carolina.

Granny Pat came to stay, letting us care for her in our home. She had no children of her own, so Roger had always told his dear Aunt Pat that if she needed us, she would come and stay. She got to that point, and Roger and Lucas went to Greenville and got her. Caring for that dear, elderly aunt was a good thing and a difficult thing, all wrapped into one.

There were lots of doctor's appointments, a couple of emergency room visits when she needed a broken bone tended, and two or three hospital stays in her last five years while she was with us. But Granny Pat helped fold laundry. She enjoyed letting little Grace play dress-up with her clothes and shoes, and Pat loved going to worship. Estuary Community Church welcomed her.

Caring for Granny Pat slowed me down to the pace of her walker. It was good for me, though I chafed at having those brakes applied to my life and my gait. But if anyone owed an aunt this accommodation, it was us. We were only paying a debt to Pat. She'd taken care of us so often.

After two or three years, Pat began suffering from increasing dementia, and I was getting overwhelmed. We found day care for her, and that was a big help. Still, overnight care was difficult. Roger's and my bedroom was just down the hall from Granny Pat's. And when she was often sleepless, so was I.

Jayna, age sixteen or seventeen, did the kindest thing ever one Saturday. Roger and I were shooting a wedding at a venue not too far from the house. I ran back home for a forgotten lens, and when I got there, I could hardly get in the door...Furniture was moved all catty wampus! I caught Jayna (her friend Naomi helping, and Barnabas too) switching bedrooms with us.

She was taking our ground floor bedroom and putting us upstairs where she had been. The point was for Jayna to take over the care of Granny Pat overnight and allow this momma to rest. I did not put a stop to what they were doing. What a blessing Jayna was—and is— to us!

Our Granny Pat got to be there at the wedding when Lucas married his beautiful Erica. But two and a half years later little Pat went to be with the Lord, just before Jayna married her handsome Jared.

After Churchville we moved a couple more times. One move was to York, Pennsylvania, where I suffered no flashbacks, no reliving the scary parts of my childhood, thank the Lord. We are now living in a simple place on a terraced acre in the lovely and cool mountains of western North Carolina. Here, Roger gets to look forward to retirement in the South. Yet, at this higher elevation, we don't have to endure southern summertime heat and humidity.

"The marriages we regard as the happiest are those in which each of the partners believes that he or she got the best of it." Sydney J. Harris, American journalist

Chapter 27: The Lord Does Know the Way

Remember that children's Sunday School song, "The Lord Knows the Way Through the Wilderness"? It occurs to me that, as I am finishing up telling our story, Roger and I have moved through our wilderness just about as long as the children of Israel were led through theirs. (Read that sometimes exciting, sometimes devastating story in the Bible's books of Exodus, Leviticus, Numbers, and Deuteronomy.) Roger and I have been married over forty years. The children of Israel wandered for forty years.

Actually, they didn't wander. The Lord's Presence guided them with the cloud during the day and the pillar of fire at night.

And, just so you know, Moses, looking back over their journeys toward the end, called the wilderness "terrifying!" (Deuteronomy 1:19.) So, we shouldn't feel like wimps when our wildernesses seem scary sometimes.

Deuteronomy 8:2 says, "And you shall remember the whole way that the Lord your God has led you these forty years in the wilderness, that he might humble you, testing you to know what was in your heart..." This book is my remembering the "whole way" the Lord has led us.

The move away from Churchville was Roger's idea. I thought I could be content to live there forever. But we'd borrowed against that little place until we owed more than my husband was comfortable with. And there was a great bargain on a new condo not too far away. Those places were selling below market value, and the prospective home was near Lucas and Erica, who were expecting their first baby! So, I agreed to put a sign in the yard during the summer.

Barnabas had moved out on his own at eighteen, and we were down to just our Grace at home. When autumn arrived, the house hadn't sold. So, homeschooling began under the additional stress of keeping the house clean-enough-to-show. When two of us were there nearly 24-hours-a-day, it seemed like a lot.

I asked Roger if we could put off selling the house and just do school. He agreed.

"But," he said, "let's just leave the sign up until the sun goes down Wednesday."

"Okay. Great!"

Of course, it sold just before sundown on Wednesday. That was a clear sign from heaven that we were supposed to move. One more time! (Or maybe two or three more times...God alone knows.)

Roger and I continue to grow closer. One way in which our delight in each other has grown surprised me. It came about during the Covid19 virus and government lockdown. We were fine, except that I found myself extra tired. This was in early May, and we'd been locked down and isolated in our home pretty much since mid-March.

I talked to Roger about us taking one day off weekly. With the strangeness of the isolated life everyone had thrust upon us, I wondered why I didn't feel rested. Maybe we should observe the Sabbath.

We adhere to the first commandment: "I am the Lord your God, who brought you out of the land of Egypt, out of the house of slavery. You shall have no other gods before me." Exodus 20:2-3

We believe that the fifth commandment is still relevant: "Honor your father and your mother, that your days may be long in the land that the Lord your God is giving you." Exodus 20:12

And the seventh: "You shall not commit adultery." Exodus 20:14. We know we must keep that one.

All the commandments are valuable. They show us the good ways which work best, ways God made us to relate to him and to relate to each other. But what about that Fourth Commandment:

"Remember the Sabbath day, to keep it holy. Six days you shall labor, and do all your work, but the seventh day is a Sabbath to the Lord your God. On it you shall not do any work, you, or your son, or your daughter, your male servant, or your female servant, or your livestock, or the sojourner who is within your gates. For in six days the Lord made heaven and earth, the sea, and all that is in them, and rested on the seventh day. Therefore the Lord blessed the Sabbath day and made it holy." Exodus 20:8-11.

Shouldn't we be resting on Saturday or Sunday each week? Setting it aside to the Lord in a special way? That was my question.

I'd thought about it over the years. But every other time I had approached Roger asking, "Should we observe a day of rest?"…every other time he'd been negative.

He was concerned that we might begin to try keeping the Laws of God as a means of pleasing him and start thinking that rule-keeping wins God's approval. While we know pleasing God has more to do with believing and loving his Son, Jesus, than with keeping the rules. Roger wanted us to be careful and guard against becoming legalistic. I wanted that too.

This time when I broached the subject, it was different. He agreed with me! We could try it.

Our first Sabbath observance was on May 2, 2020. That day the Lord gave us an unbelievably restful day. It was like magic! We have continued setting Saturdays aside, and we've added some traditional, Jewish, ceremonial observances like lighting two candles and having bread and wine with appropriate thanks and blessings on Friday evenings at sundown. And calling the day *Shabbat.*

This purposeful entering into weekly rest has been huge for us. As often as we can now, we observe Shabbat. We do it most weeks, and it gives an order and rhythm to life that we'd been missing. It's truly been a sweet means of Roger and I bonding even closer.

Jesus tells the Pharisees, and his disciples too, "…'The Sabbath was made for man.'" Mark 2:27. Shabbat (Sabbath) is a good gift. Not only does it refresh us, but it's designed to encourage trust in God. He provides. If he didn't, all the work we could do wouldn't make life better.

We attend church most Sundays in Cashiers, North Carolina, where we have found fellowship with brothers and sisters in the Lord. We've grown to enjoy the interactive nature of a liturgical service. It's been wonderful and satisfying to fellowship and pray and study the Bible with this body of believers. (Sometimes we fellowship closer to home with our neighbors at a Baptist Church.)

Though we have moved nearly as many times as the Israelis did when coming out of Egypt, I can look back and verify that the Lord has led us too. And he gives peace, his shalom. Not completely unbroken peace every moment. Don't get me wrong. But Roger and I now love each other more than ever. We have fun and enjoy each other's company. I love my life.

In 2020 we were hindered from celebrating our fortieth wedding anniversary in the manner we would have liked, due to COVID restricting travel. We still have a European trip in mind that we may take someday.

For our forty-first anniversary Roger surprised me with a relaxing and comfortable, super-clean bed and breakfast in Jasper, Georgia. Our overnight stay there was perfect. In the morning we enjoyed an amazing garden, crowded with daffodils and cherry blossoms near the B & B. Then we lunched with Roger's friends from work who live near Bent Tree.

We are happy and blessed to see all six of our children grown up. Some have degrees, all are great human beings.

So far, we have fourteen grandkids. And they are the best grandchildren on the planet. One grandson finished his undergrad degree with honors very early and now is in law school at age twenty.

We are proud of all our kids and grandkids, and we love them so much. They are precious blessings, each one—a big part of our legacy.

But God is our main Treasure, Refuge, and Delight. He is the Hero of our love story, the Lord who made us. Not only that, but he also redeemed us from the hand of the Enemy of our souls.

Psalm 116 tells why "I love the Lord"; I agree with the psalmist.

Part of it reads:

"Return, O my soul, to your rest; for the LORD has dealt bountifully with you.

For you have delivered my soul from death, my eyes from tears, my feet from stumbling…" Psalm 116:7-8

The Lord gave us a home in which to rear our children through good times and bad. And our home is where we learned to love each other. God has been so faithful. We give thanks to him for his good and perfect gifts.

Conclusion

My husband and I are wrinkled and gray now. But Roger is still smart, generous, funny, faithful, and handsome – the best! He reads the Bible daily and often sings his worship to God. (Or he sings other songs. Sometimes crazy songs! I have never caught up to Roger's knowledge of the secular songs that were popular when we were young.)

Roger no longer runs, but he works out with weights and shuns that evening bowl of ice cream most nights to stay healthy. He wears clothes well, but he's never fussy about them. His attention is away from himself and on the task at hand. Or on you. That is the definition of humility, is it not? Roger has always worked hard to provide for me. He loves me, and we enjoy such a close bond.

If our marriage could be saved, yours can too.

If this little boy, Roger, who had nine perfect attendance Sunday School pins could grow up fairly clueless about the real gospel, but then get captivated by the true and living God, there is hope that the Lord can reach you. If Roger could still be fallible and commit lots of interpersonal mistakes and sins, even though he experienced a glorious conversion...And then, if he could end up being a great husband and dad, there is no question—you can too.

If this "Preacher's kid" little girl who memorized whole Psalms and other scriptures by the time she was five years old, yet she could waver between self-righteousness and self-pity and fear—only later learning that she is safe in God's care—then the Lord can help and heal your heart. If Dana could fear God in unhelpful, legalistic ways, but then find a real relationship with God through his Son, Jesus...If she could still be dominated by anger and not even know she had that problem...If she, in that state, could be confronted and rescued, and turn out to be a fairly good wife and mom, you can too.

If Dana could be humbled and encouraged in her roles as wife and mom, being so grateful for her marriage after one year, then fourteen years, then 20, 30, 40 years – you need not give up!

The daily goal for our marriage and yours is oneness: a delighted unity and joy in each other.

God's peace to you.

"You keep him in perfect peace whose mind is stayed on you, because he trusts in you." Isaiah 26:3

"...do not be anxious about anything, but in everything by prayer and supplication with thanksgiving let your requests be made known to God. And the peace of God, which surpasses all understanding, will guard your hearts and your minds in Christ Jesus." Philippians 4:6-7

"The Lord bless you and keep you; the Lord make his face to shine upon you and be gracious to you; the Lord lift up his countenance upon you and give you peace." Numbers 6:24-26

In closing, don't forget that the Lord can make ALL things work together for good. Romans 8:28.

This is my song for that precious promise – sung to "Oh! Darling, If You Leave Me…" – an old Beatles tune.

"Weh-elll… all things,

Work together

Fo-or goo-oo-ood – Ooo-ooo ,

Weh-ehlll, all things,

Work together,

Fo-or good. Hmm-mmmm

Well, if you love him,

And he's called yoooou,

And you know

That he is the King!

Theh-eh-en ALL things

Are gonna work out

Fo-o-or good. He promised they would."

R and D. Reverse and Drive. Regular and Decaf. Roger and Dana.

Feel free to contact me at danae3@reagan.com.

End Notes:

---

[i] (Introduction) I found ways to educate myself. My chosen life has allowed me great freedom to study most things that have interested me, fitting my reading and research around my main job, that of home-making-duties and - delights.

Sometimes I have worked outside our home. My favorite of those jobs was working in sales at the Viking Sewing Gallery in Cockeysville, MD, after all the kids were grown.

[ii] For more on the nature of God, I highly recommend Nabeel Qureshi's book *No God But One, Allah or Jesus? A former Muslim investigates the evidence for Islam and Christianity*. Especially chapter 6, "Comparing Tawhid and the Trinity." Nabeel has not only taught me how to understand Islam and how best to pray for Muslims, Nabeel also gave me more insight into the God I worship—the God of the Bible.

[iii] (Chapter 2) Sin is a real danger as each of us is born knowing how to sin. And doing it…sinning. (Romans 3:23)

The term, *sin*, is a general one. There are synonyms for sin that are more targeted like *transgression*. That one is close to *trespassing*; it means going beyond a law or moral duty. The King James Bible I grew up with also used *iniquity* for a type of sin. That one is related to inequity. Unfairness.

Sin is falling short of God's standard for us.

Sin is being bad. And sin is dangerous.

The Bible warns us (and encourages us about the remedy) in Romans 6:23, "For the wages of sin is death, but the free gift of God is eternal life in Christ Jesus our Lord."

(Christ Jesus is our Master's name in English. But Jesus was born a Jew. So, his name in Hebrew would have been Yeshua. His title, not *Christ*, which is Greek, but *Hamashiach*, the Messiah.)

[iv] Before the intimate relationship of marriage, and even inside that covenant, you need not comply with something offensive to you, that violates conscience, or that you find hurtful. Pray about it; talk about it. Personal boundaries are okay.

For balance, though, inside marriage, refusing all sexual relations for week after week after month is unkind. And it keeps you from growing closer to your mate. (This assumes both are home at regular intervals, no sickness or injury hinders, and the two of you are not fasting. See 1 Corinthians 7:5 about the exception for fasting.) If the problem is that you just don't feel like it, "put on love." That's scripture. One place you can find that helpful teaching is in Colossians 3:14. Read the whole chapter.

It is important to cultivate a healthy conscience. That is done largely by reading and meditating on God's Word, the Bible. Then the informed conscience guides toward right thinking and right behavior. If you know something isn't right, you may not do it. Be like Paul the apostle who says in Acts 24:16, "I always take pains to have a clear conscience toward both God and man."

"Take pains." Do not dull the sharp points of your conscience until it never hurts you and becomes useless.

On the other hand, conscience is sometimes unreliable because it's too sensitive. We feel guilty when we did not do wrong. Talk to the Lord. Study the Bible on the topic. Get godly counsel from a trustworthy person.

ᵛ (Chapter 3) Matthew 19:9 – "And I say to you: whoever divorces his wife, except for sexual immorality, and marries another, commits adultery." Here Jesus gives one exception to the divorce=adultery rule.

Jeremiah 3:8 shows that God himself has been divorced because of adultery:

"She saw that for all the adulteries of that faithless one, Israel, I had sent her away with a decree of divorce. Yet her treacherous sister Judah did not fear, but she too went and played the whore."

1 Corinthians 7:15 – "…if the unbelieving partner separates, let it be so. In such cases the brother or sister is not enslaved. God has called you to peace."

(Regarding that verse in First Corinthians, a pastor pointed out that it's not up to the abandoned mate to figure out if the one who departed was a believer. If the spouse/former spouse behaves like an unbeliever and leaves the home, refusing to be reconciled, they can be treated as an unbeliever.

The status of their standing with God is between them and God, but the realities of life in the real world apply as people act and live.

Pastor William, our pastor at Liberty Fellowship in Seven Valleys, PA, spoke those comforting words in a Sunday School class.)

In Roger's and my story, it is good that 1 Corinthians 7:15, though providing for divorce as a result of abandonment, does not prescribe it. In the first year of our marriage, the Lord's calling of Roger to "peace" allowed him to hold out in faith for our union when I had left our home.

ⁱⁱ A very interesting article regarding Malachi chapter 2 (take time to read at least verses 10-15). The article is titled "Marriage and Divorce in Ancient Israel." It begins:

"At the heart of the Hebrew concept of marriage is the notion of covenant—a legally binding agreement with spiritual and emotional ramifications (Proverbs 2:17). God serves as witness to the marriage covenant, blessing its faithfulness but hating its betrayal (Malachi 2:14-16). The Lord's intimate involvement renders this legal commitment a spiritual union, "so they are no longer two, but one" (Matthew 19:6). The purpose of marriage as articulated in the Bible is to find true companionship (Genesis 2:18; Proverbs 18:22), produce godly offspring (Malachi 2:15; 1Corinthians 7:14) and fulfil God's calling upon an individual's life (Genesis 1:28)...

"Israelite law included a provision for divorce – initiated by the husband only. Marriages were dissolved contractually with a certificate of divorce (Dt 24:1)..."

Taken from *NIV Archaeological Study Bible.* Copyright © 2005 by Zondervan. Used by permission of Zondervan. www.zondervan.com

ⁱⁱⁱ (Chapter 4) It occurs to me that my groom was also hoping to see my best smile. Instead, Roger saw me coming toward him, coyly chewing!... Yikes!

ⁱⁱⁱⁱ (Chapter 5) There is a godly fear that we need in order to know our good Creator. Roger and I highly recommend Michael Reeves' teaching on the good kind of fear vs. the sinful kind in his book, *Rejoice and Tremble; The Surprising Good News of the Fear of the Lord*, Copyright 2021, published by Crossway, Wheaton, IL.

ⁱˣ Regarding the biblical doctrine of sin, there is some good news! The fact that sin is removeable, that it can be washed away, means that there is great hope for us. This has been brought about by the kindness of God through the incredible sacrifice of his dear Son, Jesus.

After we believe his words, agree with his assessment of what's good and what's not, we receive his great salvation! The sin, the wrongdoing, is really not intrinsic to us. Paul the apostle teaches in Romans 7:

"For I do not understand my own actions. For I do not do what I want, but I do the very thing I hate. Now if I do what I do not want, I agree with the law, that it is good. So now it is no longer I who do it, but sin that dwells within me. For I know that nothing good dwells in me, that is, in my flesh. For I have the desire to do what is right, but not the ability to carry it out. For I do not do the good I want, but the evil I do not want is what I keep on doing.

Now if I do what I do not want, it is no longer I who do it, but sin that dwells within me. So I find it to be a law that when I want to do right, evil lies close at hand."

Romans 7:15-21 is a complicated passage of Scripture that always sounds to me like a cop-out. But when we trust that God created us to be someone good and someone ruling with him in his kingdom, it helps make sense of what Paul the apostle said here in the letter to the Romans.

Once we are born again (in John 3, Jesus tells Nicodemus about this), we're not stuck with being bad, being sinful. We are forgiven!

ˣ (Chapter 9) Regarding jealousy, sometimes it is appropriate for one who loves to feel that powerful emotion. God is jealous for his people. He wants our love and admiration; he won't share us with false gods (who will destroy us when we follow them.)

The Lord warns his people against idolatry: "'You shall have no other gods before me.

"'You shall not make for yourself a carved image, or any likeness of anything that is in heaven above, or that is on the earth beneath, or that is in the water under the earth.

You shall not bow down to them or serve them; for I the LORD your God am a jealous God..." Deuteronomy 6:7-9

Jealousy is roused in the heart of God when we worship other gods. He cannot be dispassionate about his loved ones.

But for us, when jealousy twists our hearts, it needs to be confronted. Find out if there are grounds for the jealousy. Then take steps to put the passion of jealousy behind you.

There is an interesting test for adultery in the Old Testament. Found in Numbers 5:11-31, the husband who felt suspicious of his wife, finding himself jealous and unable to trust her, was to bring his wife to the priest. There was a grain offering of jealousy to be brought as well. The test involved an oath. It then called for sweeping up dust from the floor, stirring it into water, and making the woman drink.

This long passage shows that jealousy should not be ignored or swept under the rug. Though a dust smoothie sounds quite unpleasant, and I haven't heard of this measure being used in our time, this scriptural test says that we may not pretend to be okay if we are jealous. In ancient Israel the Lord prescribed a way for jealousy to be settled. Did she cheat or not? What a fearful ordeal: pass or fail for the wife, which meant life and fertility or a curse of swollen sickness and miscarriage. The priest said to the woman that if found guilty, the Lord would make her a curse and an oath among her people!

For the husband, the conclusion of the test would mean that he divorced his wife, I assume, or he accepted the verdict that she was innocent. In that case he moved forward, leading her, let's hope, with repentance, humility, love, and faith.

Song of Solomon 8:6 says, "...jealousy is fierce as the grave. Its flashes are flashes of fire, the very flame of the LORD."

Through conversation and counsel may we get past that fierce flame that only God can handle rightly. We must find an avenue to peace.

[xi] According to an impressive psychologist, maleness and femaleness are "personalities" in predictable form (although randomly evolved?) that have been "around" for a "billion years."

("Division of life into twin sexes occurred before the evolution of multi-cellular animals." Peterson, J. 2018 *12 Rules for Life, An Antidote to Chaos,* about 1 hour 50 minutes into the audio book.)

How Dr. Peterson knows that, I don't know. His twelve rules are definitely interesting and engaging. My problems with his perspective are 1) Dr. Peterson's rules are numbered incorrectly, given that the first Ten are already taken; 2) his book is grounded in praising macro-evolution; and 3) tangents that go off into the Neverland of a million directions, yet never give glory to our brilliant, Personal Creator God. Quoting the Bible, he commends it only as ancient writings. He is correct, however, in highlighting some ways in which the Bible matches reality.

The Bible's stories of creation in Genesis tell it first from God's perspective in chapter 1, and from Adam's perspective in chapter 2.

Jesus answers the Pharisees' trick question and reiterates that he created us male and female, quoting Genesis 2:24 "Have you not read that he who created them from the beginning made them male and female, and said, 'Therefore a man shall leave his father and his mother and hold fast to his wife, and the two shall become one flesh'?" Matthew 19:4-5.

Dr. Jordan Peterson and others who buy the spontaneous generation fairy-tale of macro-evolution, where the inanimate environment "selects," need the unbelievably long time frames and the unlikely, unsubstantiated theory of increasing complexity in offspring.

[xii] (Chapter 10) If you've had an abortion...if you feel regret, look for help and support. Studies show that grief and depression are common after ending one's pregnancy. One post-abortive recovery site is part of Focus on the

Family ministries, a global Christian ministry dedicated to helping families thrive. Go to focusonthefamily.com for articles and even phone counseling.

There are many places where you can get good counsel in person, including your local Crisis Pregnancy Center. There's one near us is called Smokey Mountain Pregnancy Care Center. Their number is 828-293-3600. If you're not close geographically, you can still call. Someone there will be able to refer you to a supportive center near you.

[xiii] (Chapter 12) Roe v. Wade was a poorly decided edict that thrust abortion upon the USA. I hadn't heard of it until months after it happened. I was a busy twenty-year-old mom of a six-month-old when it was passed in the Supreme Court. But I remember my horror and inconsolable cries when I found out that abortion had been declared legal. It could never have passed the legislatures of our states. So, those who were promoting abortion concocted the Roe case and demolished, with a single blow, all state restrictions on killing our little ones who had not yet been born. All at once, moms were being hurt. Tiny boys and girls were being killed. The brochure I saw, nearly a year after Roe v. Wade, showed a trash can filled with dead newborns, tossed together like garbage, their little scrunched faces so like my baby's face when he was born. I ran, sobbing, to show it to my husband. That was the first he had heard of it too.

That sad, sweeping, evil "law" doomed many millions of little kids to death. Thirty-four hundred are killed each day in the US alone. May God grant repentance for perpetrators. And mercy for the children.

We all need cleansing forgiveness because we have all sinned. Romans 3:23 says it plainly, "For all have sinned and fall short of the glory of God..."

Paul the apostle quotes from Psalm 32, "David also speaks of the blessing of the one to whom God counts righteousness apart from works: 'Blessed are those whose lawless deeds are forgiven, and whose sins are covered; blessed is the man against whom the Lord will not count his sin.'" Romans 4:6-8.

Romans 5:1 says, "Therefore, since we have been justified by faith, we have peace with God through our Lord Jesus Christ." What good news!

We have all been tricked into, pushed into, or willingly participated in things we shouldn't have done. But forgiveness is available. God can give a clean, restful heart after we have become guilty of bad things. And though the culture may tell you that sex is your play toy, it's way bigger and more important than that. Sex is designed to bond husband and wife together in the context of a covenant where both parties are safe. Neither is leaving. And sex is for having babies, optimally, in the context of a home where both their mom and dad will care for them.

You're made for greater things than trying to satisfy each lustful thought and desire that hits you. Turn from those pointless, empty pursuits that ultimately leave you sad. Jesus, and only Jesus, can fill the real longings of your heart and mine.

[xiv] (Chapter 13) Perspective is gained in looking back from my vantage point now. Sixty-something-year-old Dana can see that Roger had just come through his own wrenching, infuriating, despairing version of our first year. He needed some rest and relaxation. He needed to visit his family and friends.

We need another perspective when we get stuck. We can't wait decades for the needed insight. Our natural family and our church family can immediately provide a wiser point of view in real time. They may not share it with grace, or "the way I would," but that's the blessing. Other viewpoints are a wonderful resource. No one person can see all the needed angles.

Stay in relationship. Stay in your frustrating family. Stay in your sometimes clueless, foolish fellowship unless they quit preaching the Word of God. If that's the case, you must leave and find a different one. If there are criminal goings on or if immorality is hidden and rationalized and is going unaddressed, you've got to go.

I know the Lord can and does move us from one church fellowship to another. But if the reason for finding a new place to worship is because of hurt feelings or other personal issues, we should stay and work it out if we can. We need those who know us. We need committed people in our lives. And they need us to be committed people in their lives too. Together we triangulate, making our blind spots smaller.

Our Enemy, Satan, is always cutting in, working to separate us from our safety network. If he can isolate us, its' not long until he can defeat us. The wolf wants the lamb chased away from the flock. And that isolation is not for the lamb's good—or for the old sheep's good either.

[xv] (Chapter 18) I love *Song of Songs*, also known as the *Song of Solomon*. This love poem some see depicting the King and his bride. Others believe there are two leading men. One of the unnamed male participants represents the Shepherd who won the lady's heart, while the other is the mighty and handsome King Solomon. The first edition of the Amplified Old Testament (1962) depicts the poem featuring the latter interpretation where there are two leading male figures, the Shepherd and the mighty King. The story can be summarized as follows:

The King, finding the newly captured, beautiful Shulammite in his harem, determines to win her heart, though she longs for her kind and very handsome shepherd.

Solomon, knowing he represents the world system, writes of the one, fair maiden who got away from him, staying true to her first love. The King's rival is the Shepherd who typifies the Messiah.

I think the latter explanation fits the poem best, but you read it and decide for yourself.

xvi I highly recommend Ryan T. Anderson's 2015 book, *Truth Overruled; the Future of Marriage and Religious Freedom.*

xvii (Chapter 20) "Now it is required that those who have been given a trust must prove faithful." 1 Corinthians 4:2 NIV

xviii God speaks in many ways, though we don't always hear. And sometimes when we do hear, we don't know it's him. He speaks through his Word, the Bible. He speaks through his amazing creation. He speaks through circumstances and through others in our lives conveying his word to us. Sometimes he carries on conversations with us in our thoughts. I'm so glad he uses that last avenue. As I related in two stories of temptation in Chapter 19, the Enemy places thoughts in our minds to tempt us, often imitating our own voice, making it sound like it's only us thinking. Of course, God can speak directly to our minds too. And we can certainly learn to know his voice.

I recently read a book on this topic. Finding it biblical and well-written, I recommend *Hearing God; Developing a Conversational Relationship With God* by Dallas Willard.

xix (Chapter 24) From Day 145 of "Everywhere I Go: Learning to See Jesus" – a daily Bible-reading plan.

On repentance and forgiveness:

"...When we experience this true repentance, three things happen:

"First, our sins are wiped away. I never get over that. When we confess, God is able and just to forgive that which we have confessed. (1John 1:9) Our sins are erased, and God sees them no more.

"Also, when we repent, we experience a time of refreshing from the presence of the Lord. (Acts 3:19-21) The picture of this refreshing is one of catching your breath. When sin delivers a sucker punch, the breath is knocked out of us. But when we repent, a time of refreshing comes. Also, this refreshing is like finding a cool stream in a hot desert. It's taking the Nestea plunge—receiving the pick-me-up we need.

"Finally, when we repent, the Jesus who seemed out of place in our lives before, because of sin, now fits perfectly. He is the appointed One whose

Presence is just right. He fits exactly inside of you and inside of me..."

Quote used by permission. Lisa Noble, Administrative Assistant to Dr. Ed Young, Second Baptist Church, Houston, TX 77057

[xx] Speaking of servanthood, we need to think about how Jesus, our Master, humbled himself to serve us. Paul the apostle describes the Lord's amazing condescension in Philippians 2:3-8:

"Do nothing from rivalry or conceit, but in humility count others more significant than yourselves. Let each of you look not only to his own interests, but also to the interests of others. Have this mind among yourselves, which is yours in Christ Jesus, who, though he was in the form of God, did not count equality with God a thing to be grasped, but made himself nothing, taking the form of a servant, being born in the likeness of men. And being found in human form, he humbled himself by becoming obedient to the point of death, even death on a cross."

What a Savior! In that scripture, Paul is exhorting us to follow the Lord Jesus as our Example. Only by grace, can we do it.

[xxi] (Chapter 25) My dad was a mess in a lot of ways. But one thing I am glad he did was to take a wife, father children, and stay with the fathering project for at least a while. Even in his mental illness, he did a couple of things right.

I understand the pain that comes from finding out some of the ways in which one's dad is imperfect. But I think it might be more difficult having had no connection with him. Either way, the Lord can rescue us and reveal himself as the heavenly Father. He's my real dad. He will be yours too.

We have all hindered our kids in some way or another. My kids probably have had to each seek counsel in dealing with memories of childhood. You may be doing things to your kids right now that will haunt them in the future. But in your defense, good job! You are trying, and that's important. Be faithful. Say you're sorry when you need to (every day if you are like me) and trust the Lord.

(Now I know there are many reasons for childlessness, but if you didn't have kids just because they present a huge challenge, that might have been a big mistake. How do I say this strongly without loading guilt on people? Read Psalm 127. Verse three says, "Behold, children are a heritage from the Lord, the fruit of the womb a reward." If you don't know how to be a good mom or dad, remember that nobody knows instantly how to be a perfect at that except God. But he, in faithfulness to us and to our kids, shares his wisdom. Be brave. Have children! Then read and obey the Bible.

And if it's too late for childbearing in your marriage, ask the Lord how he wants you to love and cherish the children he brings into your life. Pray about this. All kids can use adult interaction from somebody who notices them. Someone who takes a little time to share wisdom and encouragement. These acts of kindness make a big impact on a child or youth.)

Made in the USA
Columbia, SC
23 June 2022

62126512R00075